Fo
Brittany &
Normandy

Reprinted from *Fodor's France*

Fodor's Travel Publications, Inc.
New York • Toronto • London • Sydney • Auckland

**Copyright © 1993
by Fodor's Travel Publications, Inc.**

Fodor's is a registered trademark of Fodor's Travel Publications, Inc.

All rights reserved under International and Pan-American Copyright Conventions. Published in the United States by Fodor's Travel Publications, Inc., a subsidiary of Random House, Inc., New York, and simultaneously in Canada by Random House of Canada Limited, Toronto. Distributed by Random House, Inc., New York.

No maps, illustrations, or other portions of this book may be reproduced in any form without written permission from the publisher.

ISBN 0-679-02481-6

Fodor's Brittany & Normandy

Editor: Nancy van Itallie
Editorial Contributors: Nancy Coons, Simon Hewitt, Jillian Magalaner, Marcy Pritchard, Melanie Roth
Creative Director: Fabrizio La Rocca
Cartographers: David Lindroth, Maryland Cartographics
Illustrator: Karl Tanner
Cover Photograph: Catherine Karnow/Woodfin Camp

Design: Vignelli Associates

Special Sales

Fodor's Travel Publications are available at special discounts for bulk purchases (100 copies or more) for sales promotions or premiums. Special editions, including personalized covers, excerpts of existing guides, and corporate imprints, can be created in large quantities for special needs. For more information, write to Special Marketing, Fodor's Travel Publications, 201 E. 50th Street, New York, NY 10022. Inquiries from Canada should be sent to Random House of Canada, Ltd., Marketing Department, 1265 Aerowood Drive, Mississauga, Ontario L4W 1B9. Inquiries from the United Kingdom should be sent to Fodor's Travel Publications, 20 Vauxhall Bridge Road, London, England SW1V 2SA.

MANUFACTURED IN THE UNITED STATES OF AMERICA
10 9 8 7 6 5 4 3 2 1

Contents

Maps

Foreword

Special thanks to Marion Fourestier of the French Tourist Office in New York and to Brigitte Doignon and Florence Danjean.

While every care has been taken to ensure the accuracy of the information in this guide, the passage of time will always bring change and, consequently, the publisher cannot accept responsibility for errors that may occur.

All prices and opening times quoted here are based on information supplied to us at press time. Hours and admission fees may change, however, and the prudent traveler will avoid inconvenience by calling ahead.

Fodor's wants to hear about your travel experiences, both pleasant and unpleasant. When a hotel or restaurant fails to live up to its billing, let us know and we will investigate the complaint and revise our entries where the facts warrant it.

Send your letters to the editors of Fodor's Travel Publications, 201 East 50th Street, New York, NY 10022.

Europe

Reykjavik

ICELAND

NORWAY
Bergen

SCOTLAND

NORTHERN
IRELAND

Edinburgh

North
Sea

Skagerrat

Belfast

IRELAND   *Irish*
          Sea   GREAT

DENMARK

Dublin   BRITAIN

WALES

Hamburg

ENGLAND   HOLLAND
          Amsterdam

Cardiff

The Hague

Rotterdam

London   GERM

Brussels   Bonn

ATLANTIC
OCEAN

English Channel

BELGIUM

Frankfurt

Paris

LUXEMBOURG

FRANCE   Zürich   Munich

Bern   Salzburg

SWITZERLAND

Lyon   LIECHTENSTEIN

Milan   Venic

PORTUGAL

ANDORRA

Nice

Marseille   Monaco

Florence

Lisbon

Madrid

Barcelona

Corsica

SPAIN

Seville   Granada

Balearic
Islands

Sardinia

Gibraltar

Tyrrhenia

Mediterranean Sea

MOROCCO   ALGERIA

0   400 miles

0   600 km

TUNISIA

Introduction

By Nancy Coons

Author of Fodor's Switzerland '92 *and a contributor to* Fodor's Europe, *Nancy Coons has written on European topics for* The Wall Street Journal, Opera News, *and* European Travel and Life. *She lives in Luxembourg with her husband Mark Olsen, who plays horn in the Orchestre de Radio-Tele-Luxembourg, and their daughter Elodie.*

Land of the Northmen, Little Britain. Their borders half surrounded by the sea; their windows wind-whipped by sand; their grasslands dyed kelly green by inexorable, soaking rains; their people's cheeks as red (as much from good cider as from exposure) as the apples that strain the branches in the orchards that cross-stitch their rolling hills, the regions of Normandy and Brittany— *la Normandie* and *la Bretagne*—are as closely allied in spirit as in climate with their not-so-distant cousins across the Channel. Indeed, it is in these two regions that France and England—so often primordial opposites—have dallied, warred, merged, and intermingled for a good 1,500 (and in some cases 2,500) years.

From 1066, when the duke of Normandy landed on England's shores to claim the crown, to 1944, when the English (and a few American friends) landed on Normandy's beaches to liberate their Latin allies, the two cultures have traversed the Channel—attracted, repulsed, and altogether mutually fascinated. The influence is inevitable: Just as German ways trickle over into Alsace and Spanish ways into the Pays-Basques, Normandy and Brittany feel like home to the hordes of English who ferry over to vacation there, enjoying the superior food while surrounded by otherwise vaguely familiar, only slightly exotic, charms.

Those charms are manifold: whitewashed thatched cottages; half-timbered barns; low-slung stone bungalows; wood-shingled shanties strung along waterfronts, their crooked chimneys reflected in the harbor alongside bobbing fishing boats; rose-covered country inns, their stone fireplaces ablaze at 4 o'clock, when tea is served in blue-and-white porcelain cups; windswept farmhouses, their flagstoned entryways cluttered with oilcloth, woolens, and mud-splattered Wellingtons; fashionable horse races frequented by high-born ladies wearing gloves; emerald fields flecked with cream-colored cows. Even the coveted *crème fraiche* of Isigny brings to mind silver spoons in Devon, scooping up ivory mounds.

But the mingling goes further than skin-deep; the bloodlines themselves have crossed the Channel for aeons. Bretagne, of course, means Britain—or more precisely, land of the Breton/Briton. The Britons were Celts who migrated to Southeast Britain in the late Bronze Age (from the 8th to the 4th century BC), coming, for the most part, from the lower Rhine and Rhône. By the 3rd century BC, more Celtic migrants, this time from Brittany, carried the Iron Age to England, spreading word of innovations like the potter's wheel, the rotary millstone, and the compass. By the time

Rome conquered Gaul and Britannia (modern France and England), Celtic cultures thrived on both sides of the Channel. Then, with the fall of the Empire and the disintegration of Roman protection, the Saxon hordes pressed in and the migration reversed: Waves of Britons headed back across the water to Brittany's Armorican peninsula, pushing back the Franks, who had poured over most of France. By the turn of the 6th century AD, the peninsula was so thick with Celtic-speaking Britons that they established their own combative, disorganized, independent civilization. When in 496 they allied themselves with Clovis, the king of the Franks, he felt as if he'd just claimed a little bit of England.

That privilege was to fall to another Frankish leader, of Norwegian descent. Scandinavians—Vikings, or Norsemen, or Normans—began invading the coasts of Gaul in Clovis's day; as the Frankish empire grew, amassed under Charlemagne, their efforts were rebuffed. But when the Carolingian kingdom was divided after Charlemagne's death, defenses fell and the Norsemen made inroads. In 841, under Rollo the Viking king, they took the mouth of the Rhine; in 842 they burned Rouen; in 846 they took Paris itself. Charles the Bald, from the safety of the Abbaye de St-Denis, bought their departure for 7,000 livres silver. As they continued to ravage Bordeaux, Arles, Nîmes, even Brittany, Charles the Bald and his brother Louis the German continued to pay. By 911, Rollo could set his own terms, and he settled for the region surrounding Rouen. Before long, he had expanded his claim to take in what came to be known as the duchy of Normandy.

As the Norman dukes settled their new turf, they quickly assimilated into Frankish culture, speaking Latin-rooted French, adopting Christianity, marrying Frankish princesses. If there was a vast immigration of Norsemen to the northern French coast during this era, there's little evidence of it in the dark, slight people who live there today; some theories hold that only the Norwegian aristocrats came to Normandy to mingle and beget a refined line of Frenchmen, all dukes of Normandy, all nobly named: William I (*Longue Epée* or Long Sword), Richard I (*Sans peur* or The Fearless), Richard II (*Le Bon* or The Good), Robert I (*le Magnifique*) and finally his infamous natural son, William the Bastard (and soon to be the Conqueror). Edward I, king of England, was raised in exile in Normandy—creating an obligation to its duke his country would later regret.

The story of the Normans' conquest of England has been chronicled by many, but the best and, ironically, least embroidered, version remains the Bayeux Tapestry, the wraparound needlework epic commissioned in 1067 by the brother of the victorious Norman. It was in part Edward's childhood obligation to Normandy that led, some believe, to his promising the crown of England to William the Bastard. William was the ruler of the vast terrains of Normandy, the nominal duchy that by then had become so powerful and virtually independent of France it could meet the world on its own terms. William's official state visit to Edward in England may have cemented his claim to succession in 1052. But as Edward approached death, circumstances changed: English powers began to see Harold Godwinsson, the Anglo-Saxon duke of Wessex, as the most likely military leader to save the country from assault on all fronts; William, expecting the crown, was pushed to the back burner.

When Edward died on January 6, 1066, England was in dire straits. With rebellions in Northumbria and invasions threatening, the royal council elected Harold to the throne and crowned him, hastily, perhaps guiltily, in Westminster Abbey, the day after Edward's death. To the Normans, it was nothing less than betrayal, Harold nothing more than a usurper.

To save his rightful crown, William of Normandy took action, setting sail across the Channel with some 7,000 men. He bore the lantern himself, and his own ship quickly outstripped the others; they were weighted with sleek horses, well-trained, well-equipped archers and infantry, well-mounted knights from Brittany and Normandy, and well-paid Frankish mercenaries. They landed en masse at Pevonsey Bay and built a stronghold at Hastings. Trickling south from battles elsewhere, the English forces that confronted William's men were pitifully thin: The Normans faced nothing but a ragtag mix of battle-weary troops hastily reinforced with drafted peasants and thanes swinging stones tied to sticks and old battle axes. William and his men made short work of them and left Harold the Usurper in a field with an arrow through his eye. English powers in London saw the writing on the wall: William the Conqueror, duke of Normandy, was crowned king of England on Christmas Day.

There followed nearly 400 years of Norman sovereignty in England, French in influence if not French in rule: William had claimed England for Normandy and not, officially, for France; in fact, the world began to view Normandy as an English possession under a Norman-English king. The new Norman aristocracy spoke French, of course, and while the Anglo-Saxon peasants tended what they called *sheep*, *cows*, and *pigs* on the farms, the Norman/English nobles dined on mutton (*mouton*), beef (*boeuf*), and pork (*porc*); thus the evolving English language began to blend the tongues, its Anglo-Saxon vocabulary covering the rudiments and its more complex ideas resorting to French/Latin expression. The Normans' magnificent Romanesque architectural technique—the English still call it Norman—took root; its interwoven arches and broad ornamentation was redolent of

Vikings and Celts but combined, ultimately, the genius of Rome with the beauty of French design.

Until well into the 15th century, France, England, and English-ruled Normandy battled over the lands that flanked the Channel. Philippe II of France, with the help of the Bretons, reclaimed Normandy in 1204, though England, under William's heirs, didn't officially cede it until 1259 in the Treaty of Paris. But during the endless ravages of the Hundred Years War, Edward III of England restored Normandy to France in 1360; then Henry V of England retook it in 1420, along with much of the rest of France; then, in 1449, Charles VII of France reclaimed Rouen and ended English rule—if not English influence—in Normandy. During all this changing of hands and crowns, Celtish-speaking Brittany remained relatively aloof, only occasionally joining arms with France against Norman rule; it didn't officially become a part of France until 1532.

No number of treaties and conquests could put a stop to the cultures' seeping back and forth across the Channel—a seepage that had gone on, in effect, since the first Celts left the Rhône for Cornwall, then drifted back over to name a part of Brittany Cornouaille. (Thus the Bretons and the Brits stake equal claim to Tristan, Iseult, and King Mark; both claim King Arthur as well.) Today, those Celtic and Anglo-Norman bloodlines are very much alive on the northern coast of France, from the Welsh-sounding names that pepper the Brittany map—Aber-Wrac'h, Tronoën, Locmariaquer—to the black-and-white half-timbered rowhouses of Rouen, which would seem as at home in *David Copperfield* as they are in *Madame Bovary*.

Thus the modern visitor, strolling the harbor-front streets of Honfleur, past shingled, shuttered, bow-fronted shops and fishing ships listing at low tide; peeking through Pont Aven's weathered stone fences at hollyhocks, foxgloves, frothing hydrangea; drinking cider in Locronan at a blackened oak table softened by prim bits of lace; looking across the tidal flats from the salt-encrusted ramparts of Mont St-Michel; will sense the bond, as if the Channel—*La Manche*—were but a trickle through a fissure between two masses only recently divided by continental drift.

1 Essential Information

Before You Go

Government Tourist Offices

Contact the French Government Tourist Offices for information on all aspects of travel to and in Normandy and Brittany.

In the U.S. 610 Fifth Ave., New York, NY 10020 (tel. 212/315–0888); 645 N. Michigan Ave., Chicago, IL 60611 (tel. 312/337–6301); 2305 Cedar Springs Rd., Dallas, TX 75201 (tel. 214/720–4010); 9454 Wilshire Blvd., Suite 303, Beverly Hills, CA 90212 (tel. 213/271–6665); 1 Hallidie Plaza, Suite 250, San Francisco, CA 94102 (tel. 415/986–4174).

In Canada 1981 McGill College, Suite 490, Montreal, Quebec H3A 2W9 (tel. 514/288–4264); 1 Dundas St. W., Suite 2405, Box 8, Toronto, Ontario M5G 1Z3 (tel. 416/593–4723).

In the U.K. 178 Piccadilly, London W1V OAL England (tel. 071/491–7622).

Tour Groups

Care to learn Breton cookery or explore the architecture of medieval Normandy? Then you may want to consider a package tour. Creative itineraries abound, offering access to places you may not be able to get to on your own as well as the more traditional spots. They also tend to save you money on airfare and hotels. If group outings are not your style, check into independent packages; somewhat more expensive than package tours, they are also more flexible.

When considering a tour, be sure to find out exactly what expenses are included (particularly tips, taxes, side trips, additional meals, and entertainment); governmental ratings of all hotels on the itinerary and the facilities they offer; cancellation policies for both you and the tour operator; and, if you are traveling alone, the price of the single supplement. Most tour operators request that bookings be made through a travel agent (there is no additional charge for doing so). Below is a sampling of the many tour options that are available. Contact your travel agent or the French Government Tourist Office for additional resources.

General-Interest Tours **American Express Vacations** (300 Pinnacle Way, Norcross, GA 30093, tel. 800/241–1700 or 800/421–5785 in GA) is a veritable supermarket of tours; you name it—they've either got it packaged or they'll customize a package for you. **Jet Vacations** (1775 Broadway, Suite 2405, New York, NY 10019, tel. 212/247–0999 or 800/538–0999) features country inns tours of Brittany and Normandy. **Trafalgar Tours** (21 E. 26th St., New York, NY 10010, tel. 212/689–8977 or 800/854–0103) offers a "Chateaux and Champagne" tour of Normandy. **Maupintour** (Box 807, Lawrence, KA 66044, tel. 800/255–4266 or 913/843–1211) has 14-day packages to both areas.

In the United Kingdom, **Thomas Cook** (Box 36, Thorpe Wood, Peterborough PE3 6SB, tel. 0733/332255) offers either escorted tours or packages for the independent traveler.

Special-Interest Tours *Wine/Cuisine* **Travel Concepts** (373 Commonwealth Ave., Suite 601, Boston, MA 02115–1815, tel. 617/266–8450) offers tours of Brittany and Normandy that combine wine, cuisine, history, and art, or can plan itineraries that feature one of these interests.

In the United Kingdom, **Page & Moy Ltd.** (136–140 London Rd., Leicester LE2 1EN, tel. 0533/552521) offers a cookery tour of Brittany.

Art/Architecture In the United Kingdom, **Prospect Music & Art Tours Ltd.** (454–458 Chiswick High Rd., London W4 5TT, tel. 081/995–2151) offers "Medieval Normandy," a 7-day architecture tour hosted by a guest lecturer.

Walking In the United Kingdom, **Ramblers Holiday Ltd.** (Longcroft House, Fretherne Rd., Welwyn Garden City, Herts. AL8 6PQ, tel. 0707/331133) arranges walking tours of Brittany and Normandy with walk leaders to point out natural features of interest.

Package Deals for Independent Travelers

Self-drive tours are popular in France, and **The French Experience** (370 Lexington Ave., Suite 812, New York, NY 10017, tel. 212/986–1115 or 212/986–3800) has put together eight different routes, including "The Châteaux Experience," with stays at private châteaus and manor houses in Brittany, and a 7-night package in Normandy including chateaux tours and stays in small hotels. Accommodations at country cottages can also be arranged. **Abercrombie & Kent International** (1420 Kensington Rd., Oak Brook, IL 60521, tel. 708/954–2944 or 800/323–7308) adds the option of a chauffeur to its somewhat pricier deluxe driving tours.

In the United Kingdom, **Thomas Cook** (*see* General-Interest Tours, *above*) offers packages for the independent traveler with a representative on site to help out if needed.

When to Go

On the whole, June and September are the best months to be in Normandy and Brittany, since both are free of the midsummer crowds. June offers the advantage of long daylight hours, while slightly lower prices and frequent Indian summers (often lasting well into October) make September an attractive proposition.

Try to avoid the second half of July and all of August, or be prepared for inflated prices and huge crowds on the roads and beaches. Don't travel on or around July 14 and August 1, 14, and 31.

Climate The following are average daily maximum and minimum temperatures for Rouen.

Rouen	Jan.	43F	6C	May	64F	18C	Sept.	68F	20C
		32	0		46	8		50	10
	Feb.	45F	7C	June	70F	21C	Oct.	59F	15C
		32	0		50	10		45	7
	Mar.	54F	12C	July	73F	23C	Nov.	50F	10C
		36	2		54	12		39	4
	Apr.	59F	15C	Aug.	73F	23C	Dec.	45F	7C
		39	4		54	12		36	2

Current weather information for foreign and domestic cities may be obtained by calling the **Weather Channel Connection** at 900/932–8437 from a touch-tone phone. In addition to offering the weather report, the Weather Channel Connection offers local time and travel tips, as well as hurricane, foliage, and ski reports. The call costs 95¢ per minute.

Public Holidays January 1, Easter Monday, May 1 (Labor Day), May 8 (VE Day), Ascension Day (five weeks after Easter), the Monday after Pentecost, July 14 (Bastille Day), August 15 (Assumption), November 1 (All Saints), November 11 (Armistice), and Christmas Day. If a public holiday falls on a Tuesday or a Thursday, many businesses and shops and some restaurants close on the Monday or Friday, too.

Festivals and Seasonal Events

Contact the French Government Tourist Office for exact dates and further information.

July 14. Bastille Day, a national holiday commemorated throughout the country, celebrates the Storming of the Bastille in Paris in 1789—the start of the French Revolution.
June–end Aug.: Les Nocturnes du Mont-St-Michel on Monte-St-Michel illuminate the maze of corridors and stairways of the abbey with torches every evening for a sound-and-light itinerary.
Late July: At the **Festival de Cornouaille** in Quimper, Brittany, traditional Breton music, dance, and costume fill the Place de Résistance.
Early Aug.: The **Festival Interceltique de Lorient** in Lorient, Brittany, celebrates Celtic folklore and heritage, featuring performers and artists from 8 Celtic regions of France, Great Britain, Ireland, and Spain.
Early Sept.: The **19 mc Festival de Deauville** in Deauville, Normandy, honors American film and actors.

What to Pack

Pack light: Baggage carts are scarce in airports and railroad stations, and luggage restrictions on international flights are tight. (*See* Carry-on Luggage and Checked Luggage, *below*, for exact specifications.)

Clothing What you pack depends more on the time of year than on any particular dress code. Eastern France is hot in the summer and cold in the winter. You'll need a sweater or warm jacket for the Mediterranean areas during the winter.

For the cities, pack as you would for an American city: cocktail outfits for formal restaurants and nightclubs, casual clothes for sightseeing. Jeans, as popular in France as anywhere else, are acceptable for sightseeing and informal dining. However, a jeans-and-sneakers outfit will cause raised eyebrows at theaters or expensive restaurants or when visiting French families. The rule here is to dress up rather than down. The exception is in young or bohemian circles, where casual dress is always acceptable.

Men and women who wear shorts will probably be denied admission to churches and cathedrals, although there is no longer any need for women to cover their heads and arms. For the beach resorts, pack something to wear over your bathing suit when you leave the beach (wearing bathing suits on the street is frowned upon).

Miscellaneous You'll need an adapter for hair dryers and other small appliances. The electrical current in France is 220 volts and 50 cycles. If you are staying in budget hotels, take along small bars of soap; many either do not provide soap or limit guests to one tiny bar per room.

Carry-on Luggage Airlines generally allow each passenger one piece of carry-on luggage on international flights from the United States. The bag cannot exceed 45 inches—length + width + height—and must fit under the seat or in the overhead luggage compartment.

Checked Luggage Passengers are generally allowed to check two pieces of luggage, neither of which can exceed 62 inches—length + width + height—or weigh more than 70 pounds. Baggage allowances vary slightly among airlines, so be sure to check with the carrier or your travel agent before departure.

Taking Money Abroad

Traveler's checks and major U.S. credit cards—particularly Visa, often going under the name of France's domestic equivalent, Carte Bleue—are accepted in large towns and tourist areas. In small towns and rural areas, you'll need cash. Even in large cities, many small restaurants and shops operate on a cash basis. It's wise to change a small amount of money into French francs before you go to avoid long lines at airport currency-exchange booths. Most U.S. banks will change your money into francs. If your local bank can't provide this service, you can exchange money through **Thomas Cook Currency Services.** To find the office nearest you, contact the headquarters (630 Fifth Ave., New York, NY 10111, tel. 212/757-6915).

The most widely recognized traveler's checks are **American Express, Barclay's, Thomas Cook,** and those issued through major commercial banks such as **Citibank** and **Bank of America.** (American Express now offers "AMEX Travelers Cheques for Two," which allow two people to sign and use the same checks.) Some banks will issue the checks free to established customers, but most charge a 1% commission fee. Buy part of the traveler's checks in small denominations to cash toward the end of your trip. This will save you from having to cash a large check and ending up with more francs than you need. (Hold on to your receipts after exchanging your traveler's checks; it's easier to convert foreign currency back into dollars if you have these receipts.) You can also buy traveler's checks in francs, a good idea if the dollar is falling and you want to lock in the current rate. Don't forget to take the addresses of offices where you can obtain refunds for lost or stolen traveler's checks. *The American Express Traveler's Companion*, a directory of offices to contact worldwide in case of loss or theft of American Express traveler's checks, is available at most travel-service locations.

Getting Money from Home

There are several ways to get money from home: (1) Have it sent through a large commercial bank with a branch in the town where you're staying. The only sticking point is that you must have an account with the bank; if you don't, you'll have to go through your bank, and the process will be slower and more expensive. (2) Have it sent through American Express. If you are a cardholder, you may cash a personal check or a counter check at an American Express office for up to $1,000; up to $500 will be in cash and $500 in traveler's checks. There is a 1% commission on the traveler's checks. American Express has a new service, **American Express MoneyGram,** available in France and most major cities worldwide. Through this service, even noncardholders can receive up to $10,000 in cash. It works this way: You call home and ask someone to go to an American Express office or an American Express MoneyGram agent located in a retail outlet and fill out an American Express MoneyGram (it can be paid for with cash or any major credit card). The person who makes the payment is given a reference number and telephones you with that number. The American Express MoneyGram agent calls an 800 number and authorizes the transfer of funds to an American Express office or a participating agency in the town where you're staying. In most cases, the money is available immediately on a 24-hour basis. You pick it up by showing identification and giving the reference number that was phoned to you by the person who purchased the American Express MoneyGram. Fees vary according to the amount of money sent. For sending $300, the fee is $30; for $5,000, $195. (For the American Express MoneyGram location nearest your home and for locations overseas, call 800/543–4080.) You do not have to be a cardholder to use this service. (3) Have it sent through **Western Union** (U.S. number: 800/325–6000). If you have a MasterCard or Visa, you can have money sent for any amount up to your credit limit. If not, have someone take cash or a certified cashier's check to a Western Union office. The money will be delivered to a bank in the city where you're staying within two business days. Fees vary with the amount of money sent. For sending $1,000, the fee is $64; for $500, $54.

French Currency

The units of currency in France are the franc (fr.) and the centime. Bills are in denominations of 500, 200, 100, 50, and 20 francs. Coins are 10, 5, 2, and 1 francs and 50, 20, 10, and 5 centimes. At press time (spring '92), the exchange rate was about 5.50 francs to the U.S. dollar, 4.70 to the Canadian dollar, and 9.80 to the pound sterling.

What It Will Cost

Inflation in France was low during the late '80s, around 3% annually. Air and car travel in France can be expensive (gas prices are above average and tolls are payable on most highways). Train travel, though, is a good value.

Hotel and restaurant prices compensate for the expense of travel.

Taxes All taxes must be included in posted prices in France. The initials TTC (*toutes taxes comprises*—taxes included) sometimes appear on price lists but, strictly speaking, are superfluous. By law, restaurant and hotel prices must include 18.6% taxes and a service charge. If you discover that these have rematerialized as additional items on your bill, kick up a fuss.

Sample Prices The following are meant only as a general guide, and may change substantially as exchange rates fluctuate.

Daily newspaper: $1 French, $2 foreign; baguette: 65¢; cup of espresso in a café: $1.20; cup of coffee with milk: $2; half-liter carafe of table wine in budget restaurant: $5; glass of beer in café: $1.80; can of Coca-Cola: $1.20 in store, $3 in bar or restaurant; movie ticket: $8.

Passports and Visas

Americans All U.S. citizens are required to have a valid passport for entry into France. To obtain a new passport, apply in person; renewals can be obtained in person or by mail. First-time applicants should apply to one of the 13 U.S. Passport Agency offices at least five weeks before their departure date. In addition, local county courthouses, many state and probate courts, and some post offices accept passport applications. Necessary documents include (1) a completed passport application (Form DSP–11); (2) proof of citizenship (certified birth certificate issued by the Hall of Records of your state of birth or naturalization papers); (3) proof of identity (valid driver's license or state, military, or student ID card with your photograph and signature); (4) two recent, identical, two-inch-square photographs (black-and-white or color head shot with white or off-white background); and (5) a $65 application fee for a 10-year passport (those under 18 pay $40 for a five-year passport). You may pay with a check, money order, or an exact cash amount—no change is given. Passports are mailed to you in about 10–15 working days. To renew your passport by mail, send a completed Form DSP–82; two recent, identical passport photographs; your current passport (if it is less than 12 years old and was issued after your 16th birthday); and a check or money order for $55.

U.S. citizens do not need a visa to enter France for a period of 90 days. For further information, contact the Embassy of France, 4101 Reservoir Rd., NW, Washington, DC 20007, tel. 202/944–6000.

Canadians All Canadians are required to have a passport for entry into France. Send a completed application (available at any post office or passport office) to the Bureau of Passports (Suite 215, West Tower, Guy Favreau Complex, 200 René Lévesque Blvd. W., Montreal, Que. H2Z 1X4). Include $25, two photographs, a guarantor, and proof of Canadian citizenship. Applications may be made in person at the regional passport offices in Edmonton, Halifax, Montreal, Toronto, Vancouver, or Winnipeg. Passports are valid for five years and are nonrenewable.

Visas are not required of Canadian citizens to enter France. Obtain details regarding length of stay from the French Consulate or the French National Tourist Office.

Britons All British citizens need passports, for which applications are available from travel agencies or a main post office. Send the completed form to a regional Passport Office or apply in person at a main post office. You'll need two photographs and will be charged a £15 fee. The occasional tourist may opt for a British Visitors Passport. It is valid for one year, costs £7.50, and is nonrenewable. You'll need two passport photographs and identification. Apply at your local post office.

Visas are not required of British citizens entering France.

Customs and Duties

On Arrival There are two levels of duty-free allowance for travelers entering France: one for goods obtained (tax paid) within another European Community (EC) country and the other for goods obtained anywhere outside the EC or for goods purchased in a duty-free shop within the EC.

In the first category, you may import duty-free: 300 cigarettes or 150 cigarillos or 75 cigars or 400 grams of tobacco; five liters of table wine and (1) 1½ liters of alcohol over 22% volume (most spirits), (2) three liters of alcohol under 22% by volume (fortified or sparkling wine), or (3) three more liters of table wine; 90 milliliters of perfume; 375 milliliters of toilet water; and other goods to the value of 2,400 francs (620 francs for those under 15).

In the second category, you may import duty-free: 200 cigarettes or 100 cigarillos or 50 cigars or 250 grams of tobacco (these allowances are doubled if you live outside Europe); two liters of wine and (1) one liter of alcohol over 22% volume (most spirits), (2) two liters of alcohol under 22% volume (fortified or sparkling wine), or (3) two more liters of table wine; 60 milliliters of perfume; 250 milliliters of toilet water; and other goods to the value of 300 francs (150 francs for those under 15).

Any amount of French or foreign currency may be brought into France, but foreign currencies converted into francs may be reconverted into a foreign currency only up to the equivalent of 5,000 francs. Similarly, no more than 5,000 francs may be exported and no more than the equivalent of 2,000 francs in foreign currency may be exported.

On Departure
U.S. Customs U.S. residents who are bringing any foreign-made equipment, such as cameras, from home would be wise to carry the original receipt with them or register it with U.S. Customs before leaving home (Form 4457). Otherwise you may end up paying duty on your return. You may bring home duty-free up to $400 worth of foreign goods, as long as you have been out of the country for at least 48 hours and you haven't made an international trip in 30 days. Each member of the family is entitled to the same exemption, regardless of age, and exemptions may be pooled. For the next $1,000 worth of goods, a flat 10% rate is assessed; above $1,400, duties vary with the merchandise. Included for travelers 21 or older are one liter of alcohol, 100 cigars (non-Cuban), and 200 cigarettes. Only one bottle of perfume trademarked in the United States may be brought in. However, there is no duty on antiques or art over 100 years old. Anything exceeding these limits will be taxed at the port of entry and may be taxed again in the traveler's home state. Gifts valued at under $50 may be mailed to friends or relatives at home duty-free, but no more than one package per day may be sent to any one addressee and no perfumes costing more than $5, tobacco, or liquor may be mailed. For a complete run down on what returning residents may and may not bring back to the United States, obtain the free pamphlet "Know Before You Go" from U.S. Customs Service (1301 Constitution Ave., Washington, DC 20229).

Canadian Customs   Exemptions for returning Canadians range from $20 to $300, depending on length of stay out of the country. For the $300 exemption, you must have been out of the country for one week. For any given year, you are allowed one $300 exemption. You may bring in duty-free up to 50 cigars, 200 cigarettes, 2.2 pounds of tobacco, and 40 ounces of liquor, provided these are declared in writing to customs on arrival and accompany the traveler in hand or in checked-through baggage. Personal gifts should be mailed as "Unsolicited Gift—Value under $40." Request the Canadian Customs brochure *I Declare* for further details.

U.K. Customs   British residents have two different allowances: one for goods bought in a duty-free shop in France and the other for goods bought anywhere else in France.

In the first category, you may import duty-free: 200 cigarettes or 100 cigarillos or 50 cigars or 250 grams of tobacco (these allowances are doubled if you live outside Europe); two liters of table wine and (1) one liter of alcohol over 22% by volume (most spirits) or (2) two liters of alcohol under 22% by volume (fortified or sparkling wine) or (3) two more liters of table wine; 60 milliliters of perfume; 250 milliliters of toilet water; and other goods up to a value of £32, but no more than 50 liters of beer or 25 lighters.

In the second category, you may import duty-free: 300 cigarettes or 150 cigarillos or 75 cigars or 400 grams of tobacco; five liters of table wine and (1) 1½ liters of alcohol over 22% volume (most spirits) or (2) three liters of alcohol under 22% by volume (fortified or sparkling wine) or (3) three more liters of table wine; 90 milliliters of perfume; 375 milliliters of toilet water; and other goods to a value of £420, but no more than 50 liters of beer or 25 lighters.

No animals or pets of any kind may be brought into the United Kingdom without a lengthy quarantine. *The penalties are severe and strictly enforced.*

Traveling with Film

If your camera is new, shoot and develop a few rolls of film before leaving home. Pack some lens tissue and an extra battery for your built-in light meter. Film doesn't like hot weather, so if you're driving in summer, don't store film in the glove compartment or on the shelf under the rear window. Put it behind the front seat on the floor, on the side opposite the exhaust pipe.

On a plane trip, never pack unprocessed film in check-in luggage; if your bags are X-rayed, your pictures will be ruined. Always carry undeveloped film with you through security and ask to have it inspected by hand. (It helps to isolate your film in a plastic bag, ready for quick inspection.) Inspectors at U.S. airports are required by law to honor requests for hand inspection; abroad, you'll have to depend on the kindness of strangers.

The newer airport scanning machines used in all U.S. airports are safe for anything from 5 to 500 scans, depending on the speed of your film.

Language

The French study English for a minimum of four years at school (often longer) but to little general effect. English is widely understood in major tourist areas, however, and, no matter what the area, there should be at least one person in most hotels who can explain things to you if necessary. Be courteous and patient, and speak slowly: The French, after all, have plenty of other tourists and are not massively dependent for income on English-speaking visitors. And while it may sound cynical, remember that the French respond quicker to charm than to anything else.

Even if your own French is terrible, try to master a few words: The French are more cooperative when they think you're making at least an effort to speak their language. Basic vocabulary: *s'il vous plaît* (please), *merci* (thanks), *bonjour* (hello—until 6 PM), *bonsoir* (good evening), *au revoir* (goodbye), *comment ça va* (how do you do), *oui* (yes), *non* (no), *peut-être* (maybe), *les toilettes* (toilet), *l'addition* (bill/check), *où* (where), *anglais* (English), *je ne comprends pas* (I don't understand).

Refer to the French Vocabulary and Menu Guide at the back of the book.

Staying Healthy

There are no serious health risks associated with traveling in France. However, the Centers for Disease Control (CDC) in Atlanta cautions that most of southern Europe is in the "intermediate" range for risk of contracting traveler's diarrhea. Part of this risk may be attributed to an increased consumption of olive oil and wine, which can have a laxative effect on stomachs used to a different diet. The CDC also advises all international travelers to swim only in chlorinated swimming pools, unless they are certain the local beaches and freshwater lakes are not contaminated.

If you have a health problem that might require purchasing prescription drugs while in France, have your doctor write a prescription using the drug's generic name. Brand names vary widely from country to country.

The **International Association for Medical Assistance to Travelers (IAMAT)** is a worldwide association that publishes a list of approved physicians and clinics whose training meets British and American standards. For a list of French physicians and clinics that are part of this network, contact IAMAT (417 Center St., Lewiston, NY 14092, tel. 716/754–4883. **In Canada:** 40 Regal Rd., Guelph, Ontario N1K 1B5. **In Europe:** 57 Voirets, 1212 Grand-Lancy, Geneva, Switzerland). Membership is free.

Shots and Medications Inoculations are not needed to enter France. The American Medical Association recommends Pepto Bismol for minor cases of traveler's diarrhea.

Insurance

Travelers may seek insurance coverage in four areas: health and accident, loss of luggage, flight, and trip cancellation. Your first step is to review your existing health and home-owner policies: Some health insurance plans cover health expenses incurred while traveling, some major medical plans cover emergency transportation, and some home-owner policies cover the theft of luggage.

Health and Accident
In the United States
Several companies offer coverage, designed to supplement existing health insurance for travelers: these policies include 24-hour, worldwide medical referral and advice hotlines, emergency medical evacuation, medical insurance, and accidental death and dismemberment coverage.

Access America, Inc. (Box 11188, Richmond, VA 23230, tel. 800/334–7525 or 800/284–8300), a subsidiary of Blue Cross–Blue Shield; **Carefree Travel Insurance** (Box 310, 120 Mineola Blvd., Mineola, NY 11501, tel. 516/294–0220 or 800/323–3149); **International SOS Assistance** (Box 11568, Philadelphia, PA 19116, tel. 215/244–1500 or 800/523–8930); **Travel Guard International** (1145 Clark St., Stevens Point, WI 54481, tel. 715/345–0505 or 800/782–5151), underwritten by Transamerica Occidental Life Companies; and **Wallach and Company, Inc.** (Box 480, Middleburg, VA 22117–0480, tel. 703/687–3166 or 800/237–6615) all offer such policies, differing only in their daily deductibles.

In the United Kingdom
For advice on holiday insurance, contact the **Association of British Insurers** (51 Gresham St., London BC2V 7HQ, tel. 071/600–3333) or **Europe Assistance** (252 High St., Croydon, Surrey CRO 1NF, tel. 081/680–1234).

Luggage
The loss of luggage is usually covered as part of a comprehensive travel insurance package that includes personal accident, trip-cancellation, and sometimes default and bankruptcy insurance. Several companies offer comprehensive policies: **Access America, Inc.,** and **Travel Guard International** (*see* Health and Accident Insurance, *above*).

Trip-Cancellation and Flight
Consider purchasing trip-cancellation insurance if you are traveling on a promotional or discounted ticket that does not allow changes or cancellations. You will then be covered if an emergency causes you to cancel or postpone your trip. Trip-cancellation insurance is usually included in combination-travel insurance packages available from most tour operators, travel agents, and insurance agents.

Flight insurance, which covers passengers in case of death or dismemberment, is often included in the price of a ticket when paid for with American Express, MasterCard, or other major credit cards.

Renting or Leasing Cars

Renting
If you're flying into Paris or some other city in Brittany or Normandy and are planning to spend time there, save money by arranging to pick up your car in the city the day you depart; otherwise, arrange to pick up and return your car at the airport. You'll have to weigh the added expense of renting a car from a major company with an airport office against the savings on a car from a budget company with offices in town. You could waste precious hours trying to locate the budget company in return for only a small financial savings. If you're arriving and departing from different airports, look for a one-way car rental with no return fees. Be prepared to pay more for cars with automatic transmissions. Since they are not as readily available

as those with manual transmissions, reserve them well in advance.

Rental rates vary widely, depending on the size and model, the number of days you use the car, insurance coverage, and whether special drop-off fees are imposed. In many cases, rates quoted include unlimited free mileage and standard liability protection. Not included are Collision Damage Waiver (CDW), which eliminates your deductible payment if you have an accident, personal accident insurance, gasoline, and European Value-Added Taxes (VAT). The VAT on car rentals in France is among the highest in Europe.

Driver's licenses issued in the United States and Canada are valid in France. You may also take out an International Driving Permit before you leave to smooth out difficulties if you have an accident or as an additional piece of identification. Permits are available for a small fee through local offices of the **American Automobile Association** (AAA) and the **Canadian Automobile Association** (CAA) or from their main offices (AAA, 1000 AAA Dr., Heathrow, FL 32746–0001, tel. 800/336–4357; CAA, 2 Carlton St., Toronto, Ontario M5B 1K4, tel. 416/964–3002).

It's best to arrange a car rental before you leave. You won't save money by waiting until you arrive in France, and you may find that the type of car you want is not available at the last minute. Rental companies usually charge according to the exchange rate of the dollar at the time the car is returned or when the credit-card payment is processed. Two companies with special programs to help you hedge against the falling dollar, by guaranteeing advertised rates if you pay in advance, are **Budget Rent-a-Car** (3350 Boyington St., Carrollton, TX 75006, tel. 800/527–0700) and **Connex Travel International** (23 N. Division St., Peekskill, NY 10566, tel. 800/333–3949). Other budget rental companies serving Europe include **Europe by Car** (1 Rockefeller Plaza, New York, NY 10020, tel. 212/245–1713, 800/223–1516, or 800/252–9401 in CA), **Auto Europe** (Box 1097 Sharps Wharf, Camden, ME 04843, tel. 800/223–5555), **Foremost Euro-Car** (5430 Van Nuys Blvd., Van Nuys, CA 91401, tel. 800/272–3299), and **Kemwel** (106 Calvert St. Harrison, NY 10528, tel. 800/678–0678). Others with European rentals include **Avis** (tel. 800/331–1212), **Hertz** (tel. 800/654–3131), **National** or **Europcar** (tel. 800/CAR–RENT), and **Thrifty** (tel. 800/367–2277).

In the United Kingdom, there are offices of **Avis** (Trident House, Station Rd., Hayes Middlesex UB3 4DJ, tel. 081/848–8765); **Hertz** (Radnor House, 1272 London Rd., London SW16 4XW, tel. 081/679–1799); and **Europcar Ltd.** (Bushey House, High St., Bushey, Watford WD2 1RE, tel. 081/950–4080).

Leasing For trips of 21 days or more, you may save money by leasing a car. With the leasing arrangement, you are technically buying a car and then selling it back to the manufacturer after you've used it. You receive a factory-new car, tax-free, with international registration and extensive insurance coverage. Rates vary with the make and model of the car and the length of time it is used. Car-leasing programs in France are offered by Renault, Citroën, and Peugeot. Delivery is free to downtown Paris and to the airports in Paris. There is a small fee for deliveries to other parts of France. Before you go, compare long-term rental rates with leasing rates. Remember to add taxes and in-

surance costs to the car rentals, something you don't have to
worry about with leasing. Companies that offer leasing arrangements include **Kemwel, Europe by Car,** and **Auto Europe,**
all listed above.

Rail Passes

The **French Flexipass** (formerly the **France-Vacances Rail Pass**)
is a good value for those who plan to do a lot of traveling by
train. The Flexipass allows you to stagger your train travel
time instead of having to use it all at once. For example, the
four-day pass ($175 in first class, $125 in second) can be used on
any four days within a one-month period. Travelers may also
add up to five additional days of travel for $38 a day in first class
or $27 a day in second class.

You must buy the French Flexipass before you leave for
France. It is obtainable through travel agents or through **Rail
Europe** (226–230 Westchester Ave., White Plains, NY 10604,
tel. 914/682–5172 or 800/345–1990).

The **EurailPass,** valid for unlimited first-class train travel
through 20 countries, including France, is an excellent value if
you plan to travel around the Continent. The ticket is available
for periods of 15 days ($430), 21 days ($550), one month ($680),
two months ($920), and three months ($1,150). For two or more
people traveling together, a 15-day rail pass costs $340. Be-
tween April 1 and September 30, you need a minimum of three
in your group to get this discount. For those younger than 26
years old (on the first day of travel), there is the **Eurail
Youthpass,** for one or two months of unlimited second-class
train travel at $470 and $640. The **BritFrance Rail Pass** allows
you to travel for any 5 of 15 days in France and Britain (including Channel crossing by Hovercraft) for $249 (second class) or
$335 (first class), or for any 10 days in a 30-day period ($385/
$505). You can obtain the pass from travel agencies or Rail Eu-
rope.

For travelers who like to spread out their train journeys, there
is the **Eurail Flexipass.** With the 15-day Flexipass ($280), trav-
elers get 5 days of unlimited first-class train travel but can
spread that travel out over 15 days; a 21-day pass gives you 9
days of travel ($450), and a one-month pass gives you 14 days
($610).

The EurailPass is available only if you live outside Europe or
North Africa. The pass must be bought from an authorized
agent before you leave for Europe. Apply through your travel
agent or through **Rail Europe** (address above).

Student and Youth Travel

The **International Student Identity Card** (ISIC) entitles students to youth rail passes, special fares on local transportation,
intra-European student charter flights, and discounts at
sports events, museums, theaters, and many other attractions.
The ISIC is available upon presentation of a valid college ID, in
the United States for $15 from the Council on International Ed-
ucational Exchange (CIEE, 205 E. 42nd Street, 16th Floor,
New York, N.Y. 10017, tel 212/661–1414 or 800/438–2643), in
Canada for $13 from Travel Cuts (187 College St., Toronto,
Ont. M5T 1P7, tel. 416/979–2406), and in the United Kingdom

for £5 from any student union or travel company. Cards purchased in the United States also buy $3,000 in emergency medical insurance and reimbursement of $100 a day for up to 60 days of hospital coverage.

You need only be under 26 to apply for an **International Youth Card** (IYC), issued by the Federation of International Youth Travel Organizations (FIYTO, Delta Budget Rejser, Vesterbrogade 26, 1620 Copenhagen V, Denmark, tel. 45/31311112). Providing benefits similar to those of the ISIC card, it is available in the United States for $15 from CIEE (*see above*), in Canada for $26.75 (including IYHF membership, *see below*) from the Canadian Hostelling Association (CHA, 1600 James Naismith Dr., Suite 608, Gloucester, Ontario K1B 5N4, tel. 613/748–5638), and in the United Kingdom for £4 from any student union or student travel company.

An **International Youth Hostel Federation Membership Card** (IYHF) is the key to more than 6,000 hostel locations in 70 countries worldwide; the sex-segregated, dormitory-style sleeping quarters, including some for families, go for $7 to $20 a night per person. Members can also get reductions on rail and bus travel around the world and handbooks detailing membership benefits. You can join in the United States through American Youth Hostels (AYH, Box 37613, Washington, DC 20013, tel. 202/783–6161), in Canada through the CHA (*see above*), and in the United Kingdom through the Youth Hostel Association of England and Wales (Trevelyan House, 8 St. Stephen's Hill, St. Albans, Herts. AL1 2DY, tel. 727/55215). First-year membership cost is $25 for adults 18 through 54, $10 for those under 18, $15 for those 55 and over, and $35 for families in the United States; $26.75 in Canada (including IYC cost); and £9 for adults in the United Kingdom, with children under 16 free if both parents are members.

Economical **bicycle tours** for small groups of adventurous, energetic travelers of all ages are another popular AYH student travel service. For information on these and other AYH services and publications, contact AYH at the address listed above.

Council Travel, a CIEE subsidiary, is the foremost U.S. student travel agency, specializing in low-cost charters and serving as the exclusive U.S. agent for many student airfare bargains and student tours. CIEE's 72-page *Student Travel Catalog* and *Council Charter* brochure are available free from any Council Travel office in the United States (enclose $1 for postage if ordering by mail). In addition to CIEE headquarters (205 E. 42nd St., New York, NY 10017) and a branch office (35 W. 8th St. in New York, NY 10009), there are Council Travel offices in Tempe, AZ; Berkeley, La Jolla, Long Beach, Los Angeles, San Diego, and San Francisco, CA; Chicago, IL; Amherst, Boston, and Cambridge, MA; Portland, OR; Providence, RI; Austin and Dallas, TX; and Seattle, WA, among other cities.

Students who would like to work abroad should contact **CIEE's Work Abroad Department** (205 E. 42nd St., New York, NY 10017, tel. 212/661–1414, ext. 1130). The council arranges various types of paid and voluntary work experiences overseas for up to six months. CIEE also sponsors study programs in Europe and publishes many books of interest to the student traveler. These books include *Work, Study, Travel Abroad: The Whole World Handbook* ($12.95), *Volunteer! The Comprehensive Guide to Voluntary Service in the U.S. and Abroad* ($8.95), and *The Teenager's Guide to Travel, Study, and Adventure Abroad* ($11.95); add $1.50 (book rate) or $3 (first class) postage for each title.

The Information Center at the **Institute of International Education** (IIE) has reference books, foreign university catalogues, study-abroad brochures, and other materials that may be consulted by students and nonstudents alike free of charge. The Information Center (809 UN Plaza, New York, NY 10017, tel. 212/883–8200) is open from 10 AM to 4 PM weekdays and until 7 PM Wednesday evenings. It is not open on weekends or holidays.

IIE administers a variety of grant and study programs offered by U.S. and foreign organizations, and publishes a well-known annual series of study-abroad guides, including *Academic Year Abroad*, *Vacation Study Abroad*, and *Study in the United Kingdom and Ireland*. The institute also publishes *Teaching Abroad*, a book of employment and study opportunities overseas for U.S. teachers. For a current list of IIE publications with prices and ordering information, write to Publications Service, Institute of International Education (809 UN Plaza, New York, NY 10017). Books must be purchased by mail or in person; telephone orders are not accepted.

General information on IIE's programs and services is available from its regional offices in Atlanta, Chicago, Denver, Houston, San Francisco, and Washington, DC.

For information on the **Eurail Youthpass,** *see* Rail Passes, *above.*

Traveling with Children

Publications *Family Travel Times* is an 8–12-page newsletter published 10 times a year by **TWYCH** (Travel with Your Children, 45 W. 18th St., 7th Floor Tower, New York, NY 10011, tel. 212/206–0688). Subscription includes access to back issues and a weekly opportunity to call in for specific advice.

Traveling with Children—And Enjoying It ($11.95; Globe Pequot Press, Box Q, Chester, CT 06412) offers tips on how to cut costs, keep kids busy, eat out, reduce jet lag, and pack effectively.

Family Travel Organizations **American Institute for Foreign Study** (AIFS, 102 Greenwich Ave., Greenwich, CT 06830, tel. 203/869–9090) offers family vacation programs in France for high school- and college-age students, as well as interested adults. Programs for high school students are handled by **Educational Travel Division, American Council for International Studies** (19 Bay State Rd., Boston, MA 02215, tel. 617/236–2015 or 800/825–AIFS). For information on programs for college students, contact AIFS (102 Greenwich Ave., Greenwich, CT 06830, tel. 203/869–9090).

Families Welcome! (Box 16398, Chapel Hill, NC 27516, tel. 800/326–0724) is a travel agency that arranges French tours brimming with family-sensitive choices and activities. Another travel arranger that understands families' needs (and can even set up short-term rentals) is **The French Experience** (370 Lexington Ave., New York, NY 10017, tel. 212/986–3800).

Hotels   The **Novotel** hotel chain allows up to two children under 15 to stay free in their parents' room. Many Novotel properties have playgrounds. (For international reservations, call 800/221–4542). **Club Med** (40 W. 57th St., New York, NY 10019, tel. 800/CLUB–MED) has "Mini Clubs" (for ages four to six or eight, depending on the resort), and "Kids Clubs" (for ages eight and up during school holidays) at all its resort villages in Normandy and Brittany. In general, supervised activities are scheduled all day long. Some clubs are only French-speaking, so check first.

Villa Rentals   **At Home Abroad, Inc.,** 405 E. 56th St., Suite 6H, New York, NY 10022, tel. 212/421–9165. **Villas International,** 605 Market St., Suite 510, San Francisco, CA 94105, tel. 415/281–0910 or 800/221–2260. **Hideaways, Int'l.,** Box 1270, Littleton, MA 01460, tel. 508/486–8955. **B. & D. de Vogue,** 1830 S. Mooney Blvd. 113, Visalia, CA 93277, tel. 209/733–7119 or 800/727–4748. **Vacances en Campagne,** Box 297, Falls Village, CT 06031, tel. 203/824–5155 or 800/553–5405.

Home Exchange   Exchanging homes is a surprisingly low-cost way to enjoy a vacation abroad, especially a long one. The largest home-exchange service, **Intervac U.S./International Home Exchange Service** (Box 590504, San Francisco, CA 94159, tel. 415/435–3497 or 800/756–4663) publishes three directories a year. Membership costs $45 and entitles you to one listing and all three directories. **Loan-a-Home** (2 Park La., Apt. 6E, Mount Vernon, NY 10552, tel. 914/664–7640) is popular with the academic community on sabbatical and with businesspeople on temporary assignments. Although there's no annual membership fee or charge for listing your home, one directory and a supplement cost $35.

Getting There   On international flights, children under two not occupying a seat pay 10% of the adult fare. Various discounts apply to children 2 to 12 years of age. Regulations about infant travel on airplanes are in the process of being changed. Until they do, however, if you want to be sure your infant is secure and can travel in his or her own safety seat, you must buy a separate ticket and bring your own infant car seat. (Check with the airline in advance; certain seats aren't allowed.) Some airlines allow babies to travel in their own car seats at no charge if there's a spare seat available, otherwise safety seats are stored and the child has to be held by a parent. (For the booklet *Child/Infant Safety Seats Acceptable for Use in Aircraft*, write to the Federal Aviation Administration, APA-200, 800 Independence Ave. SW, Washington, DC 20591, tel. 202/267–3479.) If you opt to hold your baby on your lap, do so with the infant outside the seat belt so he or she doesn't get crushed in case of a sudden stop.

Also inquire about special children's meals or snacks. The February 1990 and 1992 issues of *Family Travel Times* include *TWYCH's Airline Guide*, which contains a rundown of the children's services offered by 46 airlines.

Getting Around   The **French National Railways** (SNCF) accommodates family travel by allowing children under four to travel free (provided they don't occupy a seat) and by allowing children four to 11 to travel at half fare. There is also the *Carte Kiwi*, costing 395 francs, which allows children under 16 and up to four accompanying adults to travel at half fare.

Baby-sitting Check with the hotel concierge for recommended child-care ar-
Services rangements.

Miscellaneous Contact the **CIDJ** (Centre d'Information et de Documentation
pour la Jeunesse, 101 quai Branly, 75015 Paris, tel. 45–67–35–
85) for information about activities and events for youngsters in
France.

Hints for Disabled Travelers

In France Facilities for the disabled in France are better than average.
The French government is doing much to ensure that public facilities provide for disabled visitors, and it has produced an excellent booklet—*Tourists Quand Même*—with an English
glossary and easily understood symbols detailing, region by region, facilities available to the disabled in transportation sys-
tems and museums and monuments. The booklet is available
from French national tourist offices and from the main Paris
Tourist Office, or from the **Comité National Français de Liaison
pour la Réadaptation des Handicapés** (38 blvd. Raspail, 75007
Paris, tel. 45–44–33–23).

A number of monuments, hotels, and museums—especially
those constructed within the past decade—are equipped with
ramps, elevators, or special toilet facilities. Lists of regional
hotels include a symbol to indicate which hotels have rooms
that are accessible to the disabled. Similarly, the SNCF has
special cars on some trains that have been reserved exclusively
for the handicapped and can arrange for wheelchair-bound passengers to be escorted on and off trains and assisted in catching
connecting trains (the latter service must be requested in advance).

A helpful organization in Paris is the **Association des Paralysés
de France** (17 blvd. Auguste-Blanqui, 75013 Paris, tel. 40–78–
69–00), which publishes a useful hotel list.

In the U.S. Tours that are especially designed for disabled travelers generally parallel those for able-bodied travelers, albeit at a more leisurely pace. For a complete list of tour operators who arrange
such travel, write to the **Society for the Advancement of Travel
for the Handicapped** (347 Fifth Ave., Suite 610, New York, NY
10016, tel. 212/447–7288, fax 212/725–8253). Annual membership costs $45, or $25 for senior citizens and students. Send a
stamped, self-addressed envelope for information on specific
destinations. Information is available to nonmembers for $3.

Moss Rehabilitation Hospital (1200 W. Tabor Rd., Philadelphia, PA 19141–3099, tel. 215/456–9603 answers inquiries regarding specific cities and countries and provides toll-free
telephone numbers for airlines with special lines for the hard-
of-hearing and, again, listings of selected tour operators.

The **Information Center for Individuals with Disabilities** (Fort
Point Pl., 1st floor, 27–43 Wormwood St., Boston, MA 02210,
tel. 617/727–5540) offers useful problem-solving assistance, including lists of travel agents that specialize in tours for the disabled.

Mobility International USA (Box 3551, Eugene, OR 97403, tel.
503/343–1284) has information on accommodations, organized
study, and so forth around the world, and publishes *A World of*

Options for the 90's, a guide to travel for people with disabilities ($16). Annual membership is $15.

The Itinerary (Box 2012, Bayonne, NJ 07002, tel. 201/858–3400) is a bimonthly travel magazine for the disabled.

Nautilus Tours (5435 Donna Ave., Tarzana, CA 91356, tel. 818/343–6339) has for nine years operated international trips and cruises for the disabled. **Travel Industry and Disabled Exchange** (TIDE, at the same address, tel. 818/368–5648), an industry-based organization with a $15 annual membership fee, provides a quarterly newsletter and information on travel agencies and tours.

Twin Peaks Press (Box 129, Vancouver, WA 98666, tel 206/694–2462 or 800/637–2256) publishes books for the disabled, among them *The Directory of Travel Agencies for the Disabled* ($19.95), listing over 300 agencies worldwide; *Wheelchair Vagabond* ($14.95), offering tips from personal travel experiences; *Travel for the Disabled* ($19.95), which details guidebooks and facilities for the disabled; and *The Directory of Accessible Van Rentals* ($9.95), for campers and RV travelers worldwide. Twin Peaks' "Traveling Nurse's Network" provides RNs to accompany disabled travelers.

Hints for Older Travelers

The **American Association of Retired Persons** (AARP, 601 E St. NW, Washington, DC 20049, tel. 202/434–2277) has a program for independent travelers: *The Purchase Privilege Program*, which offers discounts on hotels, airfare, car rentals, and sightseeing. The AARP can also arrange group tours, including apartment living in Europe. AARP members must be 50 or older. Annual dues are $5 per person or per couple.

When using an AARP or other identification card, ask for a reduced hotel rate at the time you make your reservation, not when you check out. At participating restaurants, show your card to the maitre d' before you're seated since discounts may be limited to certain set menus, days, or hours. When renting a car, be sure to ask about special promotional rates that might offer greater savings than the available discount.

Elderhostel (75 Federal St., 3rd floor, Boston, MA 02210, tel. 617/426–7788) is an innovative, low-cost educational program for people 60 and older. Participants live in dorms on some 1,600 campuses around the world. Mornings are devoted to lectures and seminars, afternoons to sightseeing and field trips. All-inclusive fees for two- to three-week international trips, including room, board, tuition, and round-trip transportation, range from $1,800 to $4,500.

Travel Industry and Disabled Exchange (TIDE, 5435 Donna Ave., Tarzana, CA 91356, tel. 818/368–5648) is an industry-based organization with a $15 per person annual membership fee. Members receive a quarterly newsletter and information on travel agencies and tours.

National Council of Senior Citizens (1331 F St. NW, Washington, DC 20004, tel. 202/347–8800) is a nonprofit advocacy group with some 5,000 local clubs across the country. Annual membership is $12 per person or per couple. Members receive a monthly newspaper with travel information and an identification card for reduced-rate hotels and car rentals.

Mature Outlook (6001 N. Clark St., Chicago, IL 60660, tel. 800/336–6330), a subsidiary of Sears Roebuck & Co., is a travel club for people over 50, offering hotel and motel discounts and a bimonthly newsletter. Annual membership is $9.95 per couple. Instant membership is available at participating Holiday Inns.

In France   Senior citizens (men over 62 and women over 60) enjoy reduced museum admission (usually 50%) and cheap train tickets (the **Carte Vermeil,** available at stations throughout France; the Carte Vermeil costs 165 francs a year and entitles the holder to discounts of up to 50%, depending on when you travel). Senior citizens should keep their passport or an identification card with them at all times.

Further Reading

A summary of recent social, political, and economic developments is provided by John Ardagh's *France Today* (Penguin). *Portraits of France* (Little Brown), by Robert Daly, combines personal and historical reminiscences, and includes a chapter on Brittany. Pierre-Jakez Helias' *The Horse of Pride: Life in a Breton Village* (Yale University Press), Ronald Millar's *A Time of Cherries: Sailing with the Breton Tunnymen* (Cassell), and Donald Frame's translation of *Marthe* (Harcourt Brace Jovanovich) all explore the social and cultural aspects of life in Normandy and/or Brittany.

Architecture buffs should read Henri Focillon's *The Art of the West* (Cornell University Press) for a thoughtfully illustrated, scholarly exposé of Romanesque and Gothic architecture, while those who like a good thriller will enjoy Helen MacInnes's *Assignment in Brittany* (Fawcett).

Arriving and Departing

As the air routes between North America and France are among the world's most heavily traveled, passengers can choose from many different airlines and fares. But fares change with stunning rapidity, so consult your travel agent on which bargains are currently available.

From the U.S. by Plane

Be certain to distinguish among (1) nonstop flights—no changes, no stops; (2) direct flights—no changes but one or more stops; and (3) connecting flights—two or more planes, one or more stops.

Airports and   The U.S. airlines that serve France are **TWA** (tel. 800/892–
Airlines   4141), **American Airlines** (tel. 800/433–7300), and **Delta** (tel. 800/241–4141). All fly to Paris's Charles de Gaulle (Roissy) Airport (tel. 48–62–22–80) and Orly (tel. 49–75–52–52).

Flying Time   From New York: 7½ hours. From Chicago: 9 hours. From Los
to Paris   Angeles: 11 hours.

Discount Flights   The major airlines offer a range of tickets that can increase the price of any given seat by more than 300%, depending on the day of purchase. As a rule, the further in advance you buy the ticket, the less expensive it is and the greater the penalty (up to 100%) for canceling. Check with the airlines for details.

The best buy is not necessarily an **APEX** (advance-purchase) ticket on one of the major airlines. APEX tickets carry certain restrictions: They must be bought in advance (usually 21 days); they restrict your travel, usually with a minimum stay of seven days and a maximum of 90; and they penalize you for changes—voluntary or not—in your travel plans. But if you can work around these drawbacks (and most travelers can), they are among the best-value fares available.

Travelers who are willing to put up with a few restrictions and inconveniences in exchange for a substantially reduced fare may be interested in flying as **air couriers.** A courier must accompany shipments between designated points. There are several sources of information on courier deals, including (1) a telephone directory that lists courier companies by the cities to which they fly (send $5 and a self-addressed, stamped, business-size envelope to Pacific Data Sales Publishing, 2554 Lincoln Blvd., Suite 275–I, Marina Del Rey, CA 92091) and (2) *A Simple Guide to Courier Travel* (send $15.95 to Box 2394, Lake Oswego, OR 97035. For more information, call 800/222–3599).

Charter flights offer the lowest fares but often depart only on certain days, and seldom on time. Though you may be able to arrive at one city and return from another, you may lose all or most of your money if you cancel your ticket. Don't sign up for a charter flight unless you've checked with a travel agent about the reputation of the packager. It's particularly important to know the packager's policy concerning refunds if a flight is canceled. One of the most popular charter operators to Europe is **Council Charter** (tel. 212/661–0311 or 800/800–8222), a division of **CIEE** (Council on International Educational Exchange). Other companies advertise in the Sunday travel sections of newspapers.

Somewhat more expensive—but up to 50% below the cost of APEX fares—are tickets purchased through companies, known as **consolidators,** that buy blocks of tickets on scheduled airlines and sell them at wholesale prices. Here again, you may lose all or most of your money if you change your plans, but at least you will be on a regularly scheduled flight with less risk of cancellation than a charter. Once you've made your reservation, call the airline to make sure you're confirmed. Among the best-known consolidators are **UniTravel** (Box 12485, St. Louis, MO 63132, tel. 314/569–2501 or 800/325–2222) and **Access International** (101 W. 31st St., Suite 1104, New York, NY 10001, tel. 212/465–0707 or 800/825–3633). Others advertise in the Sunday travel sections of newspapers as well.

Yet another option is to join a **travel club** that offers special discounts to its members. Three such organizations are **Moment's Notice** (425 Madison Ave., New York, NY 10017, tel. 212/486–0500); **Discount Travel International** (114 Forrest Ave., Narberth, PA 19072, tel. 215/668–7184 or 800/334–9294); and **Worldwide Discount Travel Club** (1674 Meridian Ave., Miami Beach, FL 33139, tel. 305/534–2082). These cut-rate tickets should be compared with APEX tickets on the major airlines.

Enjoying the Flight As the air on a plane is dry, it helps, while flying, to drink a lot of nonalcoholic liquids; drinking alcohol contributes to jet lag, as does eating heavy meals on board. Feet swell at high altitudes, so it's a good idea to remove your shoes while in flight. Sleepers usually prefer window seats to curl up against; those who like to move about the cabin should ask for aisle seats. Bulkhead seats (located in the front row of each cabin) have more legroom, but seat trays are attached to the arms of your seat rather than to the back of the seat in front. Bulkhead seats are generally reserved for the elderly, the disabled, or parents traveling with babies.

Smoking Smoking is banned on all scheduled routes within the 48 contiguous states; within the states of Hawaii and Alaska; to and from the U.S. Virgin Islands and Puerto Rico; and on flights of fewer than six hours to and from Hawaii and Alaska. The rule applies to the domestic legs of all foreign routes but does not affect international flights.

It is best to request a no-smoking seat at the time you book your ticket. If a U.S. airline representative tells you there are no seats available in the no-smoking section, insist on one: Department of Transportation regulations require U.S. flag carriers to find seats for all nonsmokers on the day of the flight, provided they meet check-in time restrictions. On foreign carriers, ask for a seat far from the smoking section.

From the U.S. by Ship

The *Queen Elizabeth 2 (QE2)* is the only ocean liner that makes regular transatlantic crossings. However, the *Vistafjord* of the Cunard Line sails between Fort Lauderdale, Florida, and Marseille, France, in repositioning crossings. These crossings occur when cruise ships are taken to or from North America and Europe as one season ends and another begins. Some sail straight across, often at reduced rates to passengers. Others stop at several ports of call before heading to open sea. Arrangements can be made to cruise one way and fly one way. Because itineraries can change at the last minute, check with the cruise lines for the latest information.

Cunard Line (555 Fifth Ave., New York, NY 10017, tel. 800/221–4770; in NY 212/880–7545) operates four ships, including the *QE2* and *Vistafjord*. The *QE2* makes regular crossings from April through December, between Baltimore, Boston, and New York City and Southampton, England. Arrangements for the *QE2* can include one-way airfare.

Royal Viking Line (750 Battery St., San Francisco, CA 94111, tel. 800/634–8000) has three ships that cruise out of European ports. Two of the ships make repositioning crossings between Fort Lauderdale, Florida, and Lisbon, Portugal. Fly/cruise packages are available.

Check the travel pages of your Sunday newspaper for other cruise ships that sail to Europe.

From the U.K. by Plane, Car, Train, and Bus

By Plane Some of the airlines operating between the United Kingdom and France are **Air France** (tel. 081/742–6600), **British Airways** (tel. 081/897–4000), and **Caledonian Airways** (tel. 0293/36321), the charter division of British Airways.

The route from London to Paris (journey time: one hour) is the busiest in Europe, with up to 17 flights daily from Heathrow

(Air France/British Airways) and four or five from Gatwick
(Air France), all to Charles de Gaulle (also known as Roissy).
There are also regular flights—geared mainly to business-
people—from the new London City Airport in the Docklands;
direct flights to Paris from several regional U.K. airports, including Manchester, Birmingham, Glasgow, Edinburgh, and
Southampton; and flights from London to Nice, Lyon, Bordeaux, Marseille, Clermont-Ferrand, Caen, Quimper, Nantes,
Montpellier, and Toulouse, as well as from Manchester to Nice.
Remember, though, flying to France is often absurdly expensive. Charter flights (contact **Nouvelles Frontières**, 1–2 Hano-
ver St., London W1R 9WB, tel. 071/629–7772), including
Caledonian Airways' service between Gatwick and Beauvais,
north of Paris, offer the best value.

By Car   There is no shortage of Channel crossings from England to
France; all boats (and Hovercraft) welcome motor vehicles. The
quickest and most frequent routes are between Dover and Cal-
ais/Boulogne: P & O runs up to 21 daily services. The Dover–
Calais journey time is 75 minutes and the Dover–Boulogne, 100
minutes.

Each of the other routes has geographic advantages to offset
its comparative slowness. Ramsgate–Dunkirk (Sally Line: 2½
hours) offers excellent restaurant and duty-free facilities, plus
minimum fuss at port terminals; Newhaven–Dieppe (Sealink:
4½ hours) lands you in pretty Normandy; Portsmouth–Caen/
St-Malo (Brittany Ferries: six hours) can take you either to
Brittany (St-Malo) or within striking distance of Paris (Caen);
while Portsmouth–Le Havre/Cherbourg (P & O: six hours),
Plymouth–Roscoff (Brittany Ferries: eight hours), and Poole/
Weymouth–Cherbourg (Brittany Ferries: eight hours) all cater
to drivers from Wales and southwestern England.

The Ramsgate–Dunkirk service operates several times daily,
the rest at least once a day (Weymouth–Cherbourg summer
only). The Hoverspeed crossings between Dover and Boulogne/
Calais take just over half an hour but are suspended during
heavy winds and, therefore, unreliable in winter. Whichever
route you choose, it is advisable to book ahead. Prices and time-
tables vary according to season, time of day, and length of stay,
so contact the relevant ferry operator for details: **Sealink** (tel.
0233/647047), **Sally Line** (tel. 0843/595566), **Brittany Ferries**
(tel. 0705/827701), **P & O** (tel. 081/575–8555), and **Hoverspeed**
(tel. 0304/240241).

In mid-1993 cars should be able to reach France through the
Channel Tunnel, aboard special double-decker trains that will
shuttle between Folkestone and Sangatte every 15 minutes.

By Train   Until the Channel Tunnel is opened in mid-1993, as scheduled
(journey time will be slashed to 3½ hours), traveling by train
from London to Paris and other French cities means hassle—in
the form of purposeless waiting, lengthy lines, and a pervading
air of either dilapidation (British Rail) or indifference (French
officialdom). If there are no unforeseen delays, the journeys
from London to Paris via Dover or Folkestone take around sev-
en hours. The trip via Newhaven–Dieppe—offering the cheap-
est prices to those aged under 26—takes nine hours. Check
train/ferry prices with Sealink/British Rail, since there are numerous variations, depending on the time, season, crossing,
and length of travel. The faster and more convenient Hover-

craft service via Dover–Boulogne takes under six hours, but remember that Hovercraft are more affected by high winds and are relatively expensive (around £46 each way, although five-day minivacations are a good value at just around £60). There are also good-value five-day trips to such destinations as Lyon, Avignon, and Cannes. For more information, contact Sealink or British Rail.

Paris is the hub of the French train system and a change, both of train and station, is often necessary if your destination lies farther afield. There are, however, direct trains from London to Strasbourg, Lyon, the Alps, the Riviera, and the Pyrenees.

By Bus If you prefer bus to train travel, a London-to-Paris bus journey can be a rewarding experience (and costs only a little over £50 round-trip). **Eurolines** (tel. 071/730–0202), the international affiliate of **National Express,** runs four daily *Citysprint* buses in summer from Victoria Coach Station to the rue Lafayette in Paris near the Gare du Nord; these buses use the Hovercraft crossing, and the journey time is around 7½ hours. Three daily buses from Victoria to the Porte de la Villette on the outskirts of Paris use traditional ferries for the Channel crossing and take a bit longer (9 to 10 hours).

Staying in France

Getting Around France

By Plane France's domestic airline service is called **Air Inter,** with flights from Paris to all major cities and many interregional flights. For long journeys air travel is a time saver, though train travel is always much cheaper. Most domestic flights from Paris leave from **Orly Airport** (tel. 49–75–15–15). For details, check with the local airport or call Air Inter (tel. 45–46–90–00).

By Train The SNCF is generally recognized as Europe's best national train service: It's fast, punctual, comfortable, and comprehensive. The high-speed TGV, or *Train à Grande Vitesse* (average 300 kph/190 mph on the Bordeaux/southwest line), is the best domestic train, operating between Paris and Angers/Nantes. As with other main-line trains, you may need to pay a small supplement when taking a TGV at peak hours. Unlike other trains, the TGV *always* requires a seat reservation—easily obtained at the ticket window or from an automatic machine. Seat reservations are reassuring but seldom necessary on other main-line French trains, except at certain busy holiday times.

If you are traveling from Paris (or any other station terminus), get to the station half an hour before departure to ensure that you'll have a good seat. The majority of intercity trains in France consist of open-plan cars and are known as *Corail* trains. They are clean and extremely comfortable, even in second class. Trains on regional branch lines are currently being spruced up but lag behind in style and quality. The food in French trains can be good, but it's poor value for the money.

It is possible to get from one end of France to the other without resorting to overnight train travel. Otherwise you have the choice between high-priced *wagons-lits* (sleeping cars) and affordable (around 80 francs) *couchettes* (bunks), six to a compartment (sheet and pillow provided).

Rail Europe has introduced a series of "Rail-and-Drive" packages that combine rail- and rental car–travel. The most extensive coverage is offered with the Eurail Drive pass, good for four train and three Hertz rental car days within a 21-day period. The cost is $269 per person (for two people traveling together). "France Rail 'N Drive" offers four rail days and three car days within one month for $159–$255 per person.

Fares Various reduced fares are available. Senior citizens (over 60) and young people (under 26) are eligible for the **Carte Vermeil** (165 francs) and **Carrissimo** (190 francs for four trips, 350 for eight) respectively, with proof of identity and two passport photos. The SNCF offers 50% reductions during "blue" periods (most of the time) and 20% the rest of the time ("white" periods: noon Friday through noon Saturday; 3 PM Sunday through noon Monday). On major holidays ("red" periods), there are no reductions. A calendar of red/white/blue periods is available at any station, and you can buy tickets at any station, too. Note that there is no reduction for buying a round-trip *(aller-retour)* ticket rather than a one-way *(aller simple)* ticket.

By Bus France's excellent train service means that long-distance buses are rare; regional buses, too, are found mainly where the train service is spotty. Excursions and bus holidays are organized by the SNCF and other tourist organizations, such as **Horizons Européens.** Ask for the brochure at any major travel agent, or contact **France-Tourisme** (3 rue d'Alger, 75001 Paris, tel. 42–61–85–50).

By Car
Road Conditions Roads marked A *(Autoroutes)* are expressways. There are excellent links between Paris and most other French cities, but poor ones between the provinces. Most expressways require you to pay a toll *(péage);* the rates vary and can be steep. The N *(Route Nationale)* roads and D *(Route Départementale)* roads are usually wide, unencumbered, and fast (you can average 80 kph/50 mph with luck). The cheap, informative, and well-presented regional yellow Michelin maps are an invaluable navigational aid.

Rules of the Road You may use your home driver's license in France, but you must be able to prove that you have third-party insurance. Drive on the right. Be aware of the erratically followed French tradition of giving way to drivers coming from the right, unless there is an international stop sign. Seat belts are obligatory, and children under 12 may not travel in the front seat. Speed limits: 130 kph (81 mph) on expressways; 110 kph (68 mph) on major highways; 90 kph (56 mph) on minor rural roads; 50 kph (31 mph) in towns. French drivers break these limits and police dish out hefty on-the-spot fines with equal abandon.

Parking Parking is often difficult in large towns. Meters and ticket machines (pay and display) are commonplace (be sure to have a supply of 1-franc coins). In smaller towns, parking may be permitted on one side of the street only, alternating every two weeks: Pay attention to signs. The French park as anarchically as they drive, but don't follow their example: If you're caught out of bounds, you could be due for a hefty fine and your vehicle may be unceremoniously towed away to the dread compound (500 francs to retrieve it).

Gas Gas is more expensive on expressways and in rural areas. Don't let your tank get too low (if you're unlucky, you can go for many miles in the country without hitting a gas station) and keep an eye on pump prices as you go. These vary enormously: anything between 5 and 6 francs/liter. At the pumps, opt for "super" (high-grade/four-star) rather than "essence" (low-grade/two-star).

Breakdowns If you break down on an expressway, go to the nearest roadside emergency telephone and call the breakdown service. If you break down anywhere else, find the nearest garage or, failing all else, contact the police (dial 17).

By Boat France has Europe's densest inland waterway system, and canal and river vacation trips are popular. You can take an all-inclusive organized cruise or simply rent a boat and plan your own leisurely route. Contact a travel agent for details or ask for a *"Tourisme Fluvial"* brochure in any French tourist office. Some of the most picturesque stretches are found in Brittany. Request further information from French national tourist offices, or try **France-Anjou Navigation** (Quai National, 72300 Sablé-sur-Sarthe).

By Bicycle There is no shortage of wide, empty roads and flat or rolling countryside in France suitable for biking. The French themselves are great bicycling enthusiasts. Bikes can be hired from many train stations (ask for a list at any station) for around 40 francs a day; you need to show your passport and leave a deposit of 500 francs (unless you have Visa or Mastercard). In general, you must return the bike to a station within the same *département* (county or region). Bikes may be sent as accompanied luggage from any station in France; some trains in rural areas transport them without any extra charge.

Telephones

Local Calls The French telephone system is modern and efficient. Telephone booths are plentiful; they can almost always be found at post offices and often in cafés. A local call costs 73 centimes for the first minute plus 12 centimes per additional minute; half-price rates apply weekdays between 9:30 PM and 8 AM, from 1:30 PM Saturday, and all day Sunday.

Pay phones work principally with 50-centime, 1- and 5-franc coins (1 franc minimum). Lift the receiver, place the coin or coins in the appropriate slots, and dial. Unused coins are returned when you hang up. A vast number of French pay phones are now operated by cards *(télécartes)*, which you can buy from post offices and some tobacco shops, or *tabacs* (cost: 40 francs for 50 units; 96 francs for 120).

All French phone numbers have eight digits; a code is required only when calling the Paris region from the provinces (add 16–1 for Paris) and for calling the provinces from Paris (16 then the number). The number system was changed only in 1985; therefore, you may still come across some seven-digit numbers (in Paris) and some six-digit ones (elsewhere). Add 4 to the beginning of such Paris numbers, and the former two-figure area code to provincial ones.

International Calls Dial 19 and wait for the tone, then dial the country code (1 for the United States and Canada; 44 for the United Kingdom), area code (minus any initial 0), and number. Approximate daytime rate, per minute: 7.70 francs for the United States and Canada; 4.50 francs for the United Kingdom. Reduced rates, per minute: United States and Canada, 5.60 francs (2–noon daily) or 6.30 francs (noon–2 PM and 8 PM–2 AM weekdays, noon–2 AM Sunday); United Kingdom, 3 francs (9:30 PM–8 AM/2 AM–8 PM Saturday/all-day Sunday and holidays). AT&T's USA Direct program allows callers to take advantage of AT&T directly with the AT&T system. To do so from France dial 0011. You can then either dial direct (1 + area code + number), billing the call to a credit card, or make a collect call. For calls from outside the country, France's international telephone code number is 33.

Operators and Information To find a number in France or to request other information, dial 12. For international inquiries, dial 19–33 plus the country code.

Mail

Postal Rates Airmail letters to the United States and Canada cost 4 francs for 20 grams, 6.90 francs for 30 grams, 7.20 francs for 40 grams, and 7.50 francs for 50 grams. Letters to the United Kingdom cost 2.50 francs for up to 20 grams. Letters cost 2.50 francs within France; postcards cost 2.30 francs within France and if sent to Canada, the United States, the United Kingdom, and Common Market countries; 3.70 francs if sent airmail to North America. Stamps can be bought in post offices and cafés sporting a red TABAC sign outside.

Receiving Mail If you're uncertain where you'll be staying, have mail sent to **American Express** (tel. 800/543–4080 for a list of foreign offices) or to the local post office, addressed as **Poste Restante**. American Express has a $2 service charge per letter.

Tipping

The French have a clear idea of when they should be tipped. Bills in bars and restaurants include service, but it is customary to leave some small change unless you're dissatisfied. The amount of this varies: 30 centimes if you've merely bought a beer or a few francs after a meal. Tip taxi drivers and hairdressers about 10%. Give ushers in theaters and movie theaters 1 or 2 francs. In some theaters and hotels, coat check attendants may expect nothing (if there is a sign saying *Pourboire Interdit*—Tips Forbidden); otherwise give them 5 francs. Washroom attendants usually get 5 francs, though the sum is often posted.

If you stay in a hotel for more than two or three days, it is customary to leave something for the chambermaid—about 10 francs per day. In expensive hotels you may well call on the services of a baggage porter (bell boy) and hotel porter and possibly the telephone receptionist. All expect a tip: Plan on about 10 francs per item for the baggage boy, but the other tips will depend on how much you've used their services—common sense must guide you here. In hotels that provide room service, give 5 francs to the waiter (this does not apply to breakfast served in your room). If the chambermaid does some pressing or laundering for you, give her 5 francs on top of the charge made.

Gas-station attendants get nothing for gas or oil, and 5 or 10 francs for checking tires. Train and airport porters get a fixed sum (6–10 francs) per bag, but you're better off getting your own baggage cart if you can (a 10-franc coin—refundable—is sometimes necessary). Museum guides should get 5–10 francs after a guided tour, and it is standard practice to tip tour guides (and bus drivers) 10 francs or more after an excursion, depending on its length.

Opening and Closing Times

Banks
Banks are open weekdays but have no strict pattern regarding times. In general, though, hours are from 9:30 to 4:30. Most banks, but not all, take a one-hour, or even a 90-minute, lunch break.

Museums
Most museums are closed one day a week (usually Tuesday) and on national holidays. Usual opening times are from 9:30 to 5 or 6. Many museums close for lunch (noon–2); many are open afternoons only on Sunday.

Shops
Large stores in big towns are open from 9 or 9:30 until 6 or 7 (without a lunch break). Smaller shops often open earlier (8 AM) and close later (8 PM) but take a lengthy lunch break (1–4). This siesta-type schedule is routine in the south of France. Corner groceries, often run by immigrants (*"l'Arabe du coin"*), frequently stay open until around 10 PM.

VAT Refunds
A number of shops, particularly large stores and shops in holiday resorts, offer VAT refunds to foreign shoppers. You are entitled to an Export Discount of 20%–30%, depending on the item purchased, but it is often applicable only if your purchases in the same store reach a minimum of 2,800 francs (for U.K. and Common Market residents) or 1,200 francs (other residents, including U.S. and Canadian).

Bargaining
Shop prices are clearly marked and bargaining isn't a way of life. Still, at outdoor and flea markets and in antiques stores, you can try your luck. If you're thinking of buying several items, you've nothing to lose by cheerfully suggesting to the storeholder, *"Vous me faites un prix?"* ("How about a discount?").

Sports and Fitness

France has no shortage of sports facilities. Many seaside resorts are well equipped for **water sports,** such as windsurfing and waterskiing, and there are swimming pools in every French town.

Biking (*see* By Bicycle in Getting Around France, *above*) is a popular pastime and, like horseback riding (*equitation*), possible in many rural areas. Many rivers offer excellent **fishing** (check locally for authorization rights), and **canoeing** is popular in many areas. **Tennis** is phenomenally popular, and courts are everywhere: Try for a typical *terre battue* (clay) court if you can. **Golf** and **squash** have caught on recently; you may be able to find a course or a court not too far away. The French are not so keen on **jogging,** but you'll have no difficulty locating a suitable local park or avenue. The Brétons, the most seafaring of French people, will provide a hearty and well-equipped welcome to **sailing** enthusiasts.

Beaches

By far the best beaches in the region are those facing north (toward the Channel) and west (toward the Atlantic). Many are so vast that you can spread out even at the most popular resorts. The most picturesque beaches are those of Brittany.

Dining

Eating in France is serious business. This is two-big-meals-a-day country, with good restaurants around every corner. If you prefer to eat lighter, you can try a *brasserie* for rapid, straightforward fare (steak and french fries remains the classic), a picnic (a *baguette* loaf with ham, cheese, or pâté makes a perfect combination), or one of the fast-food joints that have mushroomed in cities and towns over recent years. Snack possibilities—from pastry shops (*patisseries*) to pancake/roast chestnut street sellers—are legion.

French breakfasts are relatively skimpy: good coffee, fruit juice if you request it, bread, butter, and croissants. You can "breakfast" in cafés as well as hotels. If you're in the mood for bacon and eggs, however, you're in trouble.

Mealtimes Dinner is the main meal and usually begins at 8 PM. Lunch—starting at 12:30 or 1—can be as copious as you care to make it.

Precautions Tap water is safe, though not always appetizing. Mineral water—there is a vast choice of both still (*eau plate*) and fizzy (*eau gazeuse*)—is a palatable alternative. Perhaps the biggest eating problem in France is saying no: If you're invited to a French family's home, you will be encouraged, if not expected, to take two or three servings of everything offered.

Ratings Highly recommended restaurants are indicated by a star ★.

Category	Cost*: Major City	Cost*: Other Areas
Very Expensive	over 500 francs	over 400 francs
Expensive	250–500 francs	200–400 francs
Moderate	150–250 francs	100–200 francs
Inexpensive	under 150 francs	under 100 francs

*per person for a three-course meal, including tax (18.6%) and tip but not wine

Lodging

Normandy and Brittany have a wide range of accommodations, ranging from rambling old village inns that cost next to nothing to stylish converted châteaus that cost the earth. Prices must, by law, be posted at the hotel entrance and should include taxes and service. Prices are always by room, not per person (ask for a *grand lit* if you want a double bed). Breakfast is not always included in this price, but you are usually expected to have it and are often charged for it regardless. In smaller rural hotels you may be expected to have your evening meal at the hotel, too.

Hotels Hotels are officially classified from one-star up to four-star/deluxe. France is not dominated by big hotel chains; examples in the upper price bracket include **Frantel, Holiday Inn, Novotel,** and **Sofitel.** The **Ibis** and **Climat de France** chains are more moderately priced; the new **Formula 1** chain provides basic comfort for up to three persons per room for 135 francs a night. Chain hotels, as a rule, lack atmosphere, with the following exceptions: **Logis de France** has small, inexpensive hotels that can be relied on for minimum standards of comfort, character, and regional cuisine. Watch for the distinctive yellow-and-green signs. The Logis de France paperback guide is widely available in bookshops (cost: around 65 francs) or from Logis de France, 83 av. d'Italie, 75013 Paris. **France-Accueil** is another friendly, low-cost chain (free booklet from France-Accueil, 85 rue Dessous-des-Berges, 75013 Paris). You can stay in style at any of the 150 members of the prestigious **Relais & Châteaux** chain of converted châteaus and manor houses. Each hotel is distinctively furnished, provides top cuisine, and often stands in spacious grounds. A booklet listing members is available in bookshops or from Relais & Châteaux (9 av. Marceau, 75016 Paris).

Self-catering Best bets are the **Gîtes Ruraux,** which offer a family or group the possibility of a low-cost, self-catering vacation in a furnished cottage, chalet, or apartment in the country; rentals are by the week or month. For details contact either the **Maison des Gîtes de France** (35 rue Godot-de-Mauroy, 75009 Paris, tel. 47–42–20–20), naming which region interests you, or the **French Government Tourist Office** in London (178 Piccadilly, W1V OAL, tel. 01/491–7622), which runs a special reservation service.

Bed and Breakfast Bed-and-breakfasts, known in France as *Chambres d'Hôte,* are becoming increasingly popular, especially in rural areas. Check local tourist offices for details.

Youth Hostels Given that cheap hotel accommodations in France are so easy to find, there is scarcely any economic reason for staying in a youth hostel, especially since standards in France don't measure up to those in neighboring countries. If you enjoy a hostel ambience, however, you may care to note the address of the French headquarters (**Fédération Unie des Auberges de Jeunesse,** 10 rue Notre-Dame-de-Lorette, 75009 Paris).

Villas The French Government Tourist Offices in New York and London publish extensive lists of agencies specializing in villa rentals. You may also write to **Rent-a-Villa Ltd.** (3 W. 51st St., New York, NY 10019) or, in France, **Interhome** (15 av. Jean-Aicard, 75011 Paris).

Camping French campsites have a high reputation for organization and amenities, but they tend to be jam-packed in July and August. More and more campsites now welcome advance reservations; if you're traveling in summer, it makes good sense to book ahead. A guide to the country's campsites is published by the **Fédération Française de Camping et de Caravaning** (78 rue de Rivoli, 75004 Paris).

Ratings Highly recommended hotels are indicated by a star ★.

Category	Cost*: Major City	Cost*: Other Areas
Very Expensive	over 1,000 francs	over 800 francs
Expensive	600–1,000 francs	400–800 francs

Moderate	300–600 francs	200–400 francs
Inexpensive	under 300 francs	under 200 francs

All prices are for a standard double room for two, including tax (18.6%) and service charge.

Credit Cards

The following credit card abbreviations are used: AE, American Express; DC, Diners Club; MC, MasterCard; and V, Visa.

2 Portraits of Brittany & Normandy

Brittany and Normandy at a Glance: A Chronology

c 3500 BC Megalithic stone complexes erected at Carnac, Brittany

after 500 BC Celts appear in France

58–51 BC Julius Caesar conquers Gaul; writes up the war in *De Bello Gallico*

52 BC Lutetia, later to become Paris, is built by the Gallo-Romans

AD 212 Roman citizenship conferred on all free inhabitants of Gaul

406 Invasion by the Vandals (Germanic tribes)

c 500 Britons driven from Britain by Anglo-Saxons settle in Brittany (part of ancient Armorica)

The Merovingian Dynasty

486–511 Clovis, king of the Franks (481–511), defeats the Roman governor of Gaul and founds the Merovingian Dynasty

497 Franks converted to Christianity

567 The Frankish kingdom is divided into three parts—the eastern countries (Austrasia), later to become Belgium and Germany; the western countries (Neustria), later to become France; and Burgundy

The Carolingian Dynasty

768–778 Charlemagne (768–814) becomes king of the Franks (768)

c 782 Carolingian renaissance in art, architecture, and education

800 The pope crowns Charlemagne Holy Roman Emperor in Rome

820 Norse invasions begin

814–987 Death of Charlemagne. The Carolingian line continues until 987 through a dozen or so monarchs, with a batch called Charles (the Bald, the Fat, the Simple) and a sprinkling of Louis

911 Norse leader Rollo receives region around mouth of Seine as fief from Frankish king

c 950 In Norman territory, extended by additions after 911, Norman language no longer spoken at Rouen. French language and Christianity spread throughout Normandy

The Capetian Dynasty

987 Hugh Capet (987–996) is elected king of France and establishes the principle of hereditary rule for his descendants

1066 Conquest of England by William, duke of Normandy (1066–87)

1067 Work begins on the Bayeux Tapestry, the Romanesque work of art celebrating the Norman Conquest

1140   The Gothic style of architecture first appears at St-Denis and later becomes fully developed at the cathedrals of Chartres, Reims, Amiens, and Notre-Dame in Paris

c 1150   Struggle between the Anglo-Norman kings (Angevin Empire) and the French

1204   Normandy conquered and annexed to France by Philip Augustus

1302–07 Philippe IV (1285–1314), the Fair, calls together the first States-General, predecessor to the French Parliament. He disbands the Knights Templars to gain their wealth (1307)

The Valois Dynasty

1337–1453 Hundred Years' War between France and England: English reconquer Normandy but lose it again in 1450

1348–1350 The Black Death rages in France

1453   France finally defeats England, terminating the Hundred Years' War and the English claim to the French throne

1515–47 Reign of François I, who imports Italian artists, including Leonardo da Vinci (1452–1519), and brings the Renaissance to France

1532   Duchy of Brittany formally incorporated into France

1558   France captures Calais, England's last territory on French soil

1562–98 Wars of Religion (Catholics versus Protestants/Huguenots) within France

The Bourbon Dynasty

1589   The first Bourbon king, Henri IV (1589–1610), is a Huguenot who converts to Catholicism and achieves peace in France. He signs the Edict of Nantes, giving limited freedom of worship to Protestants

1643–1715 Reign of Louis XIV, the Sun King, an absolute monarch who builds the Baroque power base of Versailles and presents Europe with a glorious view of France

1660   Classical period of French culture: writers Molière (1622–73), Jean Racine (1639–99), Pierre Corneille (1606–84), and painter Nicolas Poussin (1594–1665)

1776   The French assist in the American War of Independence. Ideals of liberty cross the Atlantic with the returning troops to reinforce new social concepts

The French Revolution

1789–1804 The Bastille is stormed on July 14, 1789. Following upon early Republican ideals comes the Terror and the administration of the Directory under Robespierre. There are widespread political executions—Louis XVI and his queen, Marie Antoinette, are guillotined in 1793. Reaction sets in, and the instigators of the Terror are themselves executed (1794). Napoleon Bonaparte enters the scene as the champion of the Directory (1795–99) and is installed as First Consul during the Consulate (1799–1804)

1791 Normandy divided into departments of Orne, Calvados, Manche, Eure, and Seine-Inférieure; Brittany's departments are Ille-et-Vilaine, Côtes-du-Nord, Finistère, Morbihan, and Loire-Maritime

The First Empire

1804 Napoleon crowns himself Emperor of France at Notre-Dame in the presence of the pope

1805–12 Napoleon conquers most of Europe. The Napoleonic Age is marked by a neoclassical style in the arts, called Empire, as well as by the rise of Romanticism—characterized by such writers as Chateaubriand (1768–1848) and Stendhal (1783–1842), and the painters Eugène Delacroix (1798–1863) and Théodore Géricault (1791–1824)—which is to dominate the arts of the 19th century

1812–14 Winter cold and Russian determination defeat Napoleon outside Moscow. The emperor abdicates and is transported to Elba in the Mediterranean (1814)

Restoration of the Bourbons

1814–15 Louis XVIII, brother of the executed Louis XVI, regains the throne after the Congress of Vienna is held to settle peace terms

1815 The Hundred Days: Napoleon returns from Elba and musters an army on his march to the capital, but lacks national support. He is defeated at Waterloo (June 18) and exiled to the island of St. Helena in the South Atlantic

1821 Napoleon dies in exile

1830 Bourbon king Charles X, locked into a prerevolutionary state of mind, abdicates. A brief upheaval (Three Glorious Days) brings Louis-Philippe, the Citizen King, to the throne

1846–48 Severe industrial and farming depression contribute to Louis-Philippe's abdication (1848)

Second Republic and Second Empire

1848–52 Louis-Napoleon (nephew and step-grandson of Napoleon I) is elected president of the short-lived Second Republic. He makes a successful attempt to assume supreme power and is declared emperor of France, taking the title Napoleon III

The Third Republic

1870–71 The Franco-Prussian War sees Paris besieged, and France loses Alsace and Lorraine to Prussia before the peace treaty is signed

1871–1914 Before World War I, France expands her industries and builds up a vast colonial empire in North Africa and Southeast Asia

1874 Emergence of the Impressionist school of painting: Monet, Pierre Auguste Renoir (1841–1919), and Edgar Degas (1834–1917)

1904 The Entente Cordiale: England and France become firm allies

1914–18 During World War I, France fights with the Allies, opposing Germany, Austria-Hungary, and Turkey. With the Treaty of Versailles (1919), France regains Alsace and Lorraine and attempts to exact financial and economic reparations from Germany

1918–39 Between wars, France attracts artists and writers, including Americans—Ernest Hemingway (1899–1961) and Gertrude Stein (1874–1946)

1939–45 At the beginning of World War II, France fights with the Allies until invaded and defeated by Germany in 1940. Breton autonomists resist German bids for collaboration

1944 D-Day, June 6: The Allies land on the beaches of Normandy and successfully invade France

1944–46 A provisional government takes power under General de Gaulle; American aid assists French recovery

The Fourth Republic

1946 France adopts a new constitution; French women gain the right to vote

1946–54 In the Indochinese War, France is unable to regain control of her colonies in Southeast Asia

1954–62 The Algerian Revolution achieves Algeria's independence from France. Thereafter, other French African colonies gain independence

1957 The Treaty of Rome establishes the European Economic Community (now known as the European Community—EC), with France a founding member

The Fifth Republic

1958–68 De Gaulle is the first president under a new constitution

1976 The first supersonic transatlantic passenger service begins with the Anglo-French Concorde

1981 François Mitterrand is elected the first Socialist president of France since World War II

1988 Mitterrand is elected for a second term

1989 Bicentennial celebration of the French Revolution

1990 TGV train clocks a world record—515 kph (322 mph)—on a practice run. Channel Tunnel link-up between French and English workers

A Good Day's Feast

By Nancy Coons *The [wedding] table had been set up in the carriage shed. On it lay four full sirloin roasts, six chicken fricassées, veal casserole, three entire legs of lamb and, in the middle, a lovely roast suckling pig, flanked by four andouilles à l'oseille [chitterling sausage with sorrel]. At the corners stood carafes of eau-de-vie. Bottles of sweet cider oozed thick foam around their corks, and all the glasses had been filled to the brim in advance. Great platters of custard, which quivered at the least jostle to the table, had been inscribed with the initials of the newlyweds in arabesques of nonpareilles. . . . Until nightfall, they ate. When they were too weary of sitting, they went walking in the barnyard or played a game of cork in the barn, then went back to the table. Some, near the end, fell asleep and snored. But, after the coffee, everything came back to life; then they tried a song or feats of strength, lifted weights, attempted to pass their head under their arm while holding the thumb on the table, tried to raise carts onto shoulders, told risqué stories, kissed the ladies. At night, when it was time to leave, the horses—gorged to the nostrils with oats—could barely fit between the shafts; they kicked, bucked, and broke their harnesses; their masters swore or laughed and all night, in the moonlight, by the country roads, there were runaway carriages that raced at full gallop, bounding over ditches, leaping over gravel heaps, catching on embankments, with women leaning out, trying to grab the reins.*

> *Madame Bovary*, by Gustave Flaubert,
> set in the Caux region of Normandy

If Normandy and Brittany's reputation for great gastronomy falls short of those of the Dordogne, Alsace, or Provence, no one rivals them for culinary excess. Another midday menu recorded by George M. Musgrave in his 1855 *A Ramble through Normandy:* soup, fried mackerel, beefsteak, beans, fried potatoes; then an omelet *fines herbes*, a veal stew, a roast chicken with mushrooms, and ham hock with spinach; then apricot tart, custards, and endive salad; then a small roast leg of lamb, followed by coffee, absinthe, cheese, pears, plums, grapes, and cakes. Dinner for two *à la Normande*.

Yet these early, meaty meals might seem barren by modern Norman standards, where rich dairy cream thickens every sauce and butter goes down less by the pat than by the slab. In fact, despite its proximity to the Channel and the heaps of seafood that are carted to central France from its shores, Normandy makes its name in the world less for its fish than for its dairy products—its vats of creamy sweet butter, its inimitable Isigny *crème fraiche*, and its famous cheeses—

Pont-l'Eveque, Liverot, and, of course, the ubiquitous and only truly authentic Camembert. Even Gervais Petit Suisse, those tiny commercial fruit-flavored *fromages frais* sold in colorful sixpacks (picnickers take note) come from Normandy. The one seafood specialty that showcases the region's finest catch-of-the-day—*sole à la Normande*—smothers its garnish of crayfish, oysters, prawns, and mushrooms with thick local cream.

There are yet other sources of richness native to Normandy: From that great city where Joan of Arc was tried and burned at the stake and where Mme. Bovary erred in a close-shuttered carriage, *Caneton Rouennais* (Rouen duck) is strangled to preserve the precious blood that's pressed out to thicken the sauce. (The unfortunate creatures make excellent pâtés, too.) *Tripes à la mode de Caen*, from another Norman capital, stews all day in a rich brew of ox feet, Calvados, and savory vegetables; *andouilles* (pork sausages) are often lightly smoked.

The seafood served up in coast towns rivals any in France—rosy langoustines, delicate sole, batlike skate, silver smelt, and mackerel, their iridescent tiger stripes forming dazzling patterns in the fish market bins. *Moules* (mussels) from Normandy, by French standards, surpass the fleshier North Sea version marketed out of Holland for flavor and tenderness; they, too, are often smothered in Norman cream.

All this heavy diet calls for a good *digestif*, and Calvados—Normandy's apple-perfumed brandy—goes down so well the Normans made two places for it in the mealtime ritual: once at the end, of course, after coffee; but also half-way through the menu—between the tripe and roast veal, perhaps. This is known as the *trou Normand* or the "hole"—whether in the meal or in the diner's stomach depends on the quality of the Calvados. Good Calvados captures the very essence of the apples that cover the inland regions of Normandy, and so does the tangy local cider, light on alcohol and an excellent accompaniment for meat-heavy meals.

One of the best known specialties of the region owes as much to Brittany as to Normandy: Mère Poulard's famous omelets, whipped to double-size and cooked in a great stone fireplace, come from Mont St-Michel, which both regions claim as their own. (One diplomat suggests that at high tide, when it's an island, it belongs to Normandy's coast; at low tide, a causeway connects it to Brittany.) When in 1932 a journalist from *La Table* magazine asked Mme. Poulard for the secret to her flawless, airy omelets, she wrote in reply: "I break some good eggs in a bowl, I beat them well, I put a good piece of butter in the pan, I throw the eggs into it, and I shake it constantly. I am happy, monsieur, if this recipe pleases you."

Despite its proximity to Normandy, Brittany and its cuisine have a personality all their own. As if the harvest of the salt fields had seeped into the cows' grass and hay, Breton butter is served salted—and in generous quantity, even on the Nantes *tartine de beurre* (butter sandwich) eaten with the fruit at the end of the meal. The salt of the earth does, in fact, seep into the meat of the lambs raised on the *pré-salé* (salt flats), producing the most sought-after *gigot* (leg of lamb) in France. In Brittany it's usually roasted with garlic and served with long, white *haricots* (beans), simmered with onion, tomato, and the juices of the gigot.

But Brittany, with most of its border exposed to the North Atlantic, relies more on seafood than its Norman neighbor. Less well-known than its southern cousin *bouillabaisse*, the Breton fish stew is called *cortriade*, and—like its counterpart—it makes the most of whatever sea dwellers are left in the fisherman's net. Sole, mackerel, whiting (*merlan*), mullet (*rouget*), and langoustines often dominate the dish, but the key distinction between a cortriade and a true bouillabaisse is the presence of those tender little North Atlantic mussels and the very local *palourdes*—delicate, ivory-shelled clams.

Not to be missed in season are the region's famous *belon* and *fine de claire* oysters, found in months with the letter "R" (all but June, July, and August) and best consumed fresh, raw, and—if budget allows—by the dozens. Brittany used to be the capital of the sardine industry, when millions of the tiny fish were hauled in, salted down on the boat, then beheaded and gutted by hand, dried on an iron grill over a wood fire, boiled in copper cauldrons full of oil, and laid in layers in tins that were soldered shut and shipped around the world. Nowadays most of the tinned sardines you buy come from Portugal or elsewhere, but local, fresh sardines can still be found in Breton markets.

Probably the best-known delicacy of Brittany is its *galette de sarrassin* or buckwheat crêpe, an elastic pancake most often served with savory accompaniments—fried egg, bacon, or just plain salted butter—and often washed down with buttermilk. For travelers who like to eat lightly once a day, they offer an opportunity (rare in France) for a small, quick lunch. But their universal dessert counterpart, made with white wheat flour and served with the usual array of sugar, butter, whipped cream, or chocolate syrup, is difficult to resist.

A dessert more authentic to the region, though, would be the solid gold *gateau Breton*, a staunch, rich butter-cookie of a cake stamped with ornate patterns. Its straightforward ingredients: nothing but egg yolks, flour, sugar, and salted butter. They are sold in all sizes in pastry and snack shops, stacked like golden coins in display bins.

While wine is widely available throughout both Brittany and Normandy, both regions continue to cultivate their own, home-grown cider. In fact, for generations Brittany has had a reputation for heavy drinking—another variation in lifestyle that binds it more closely with its ancient relatives across the Channel than with its Latin-rooted compatriots. Their beverage of choice: Good strong cider and orchard-fruit *eaux de vie*.

Either drink goes down smoothly enough on a typical Breton day, with the cold, damp wind whipping in from the ocean and the dark, carved furniture reflecting the firelight. In fact, it may be the harsh climate of the North Atlantic coastline as much as the bounty of the sea, orchards, and pastures that inspire both Normandy and Brittany's regional pastime: gathering by the old stone hearth for good food, for good drink, for good company—in short, for a good day's feast.

3 Normandy

Rouen to Mont-St-Michel

Normandy (or Normandie, as the French spell it), the coastal region lying northwest of Paris, probably has more associations for English-speaking visitors than does any other part of France. William the Conqueror, Joan of Arc, the Bayeux Tapestry, and the D-Day landing beaches have become household names in English, just as they have in French.

Normandy is one of the country's finest gastronomic regions, producing excellent cheeses, such as Camembert, and Calvados, a powerful apple brandy. The area has become popular with British vacationers not only because it's right across the Channel but also because of its charming countryside, from the wild, granite cliffs in the west to the long sandy beaches along the Channel coast, from the wooded valleys of the south to the lush green meadows and apple orchards in the center.

Historic buildings—castles, churches, and monuments—crown the Norman countryside as reminders of its rich and eventful past. Following the 1066 invasion of England by the Norman duke, William (the Conqueror), Normandy switched between English and French dominion for several centuries. In Rouen in 1431, Joan of Arc was burned at the stake, marking a turning point in the Hundred Years' War, the last major medieval conflict between the French and the English. The most celebrated building in Normandy is the abbey of Mont-St-Michel, erected on a 264-foot mound of granite cut off from the mainland at high tide; it's an architectural marvel and the most visited site in provincial France.

Normandy features 375 miles of coastline bordering the English Channel, four major ports—Le Havre, Rouen, Dieppe, and Cherbourg—and coastal towns with seafaring pasts, such as Honfleur, with its picturesque old harbor, and former fishing villages like Fécamp. Sandwiched between are the beaches of such fashionable resorts as Deauville, Cabourg, and Etretat, where visitors can be found reclining in deck chairs, gin and tonic in hand.

Essential Information

Important Addresses and Numbers

Tourist Information Each of Normandy's five *départements* has its own central tourist office: **Alençon** (Orne, 88 rue St-Blaise, tel. 33–28–88–71), **Caen** (Calvados, pl. du Canada, tel. 31–86–53–30), **Evreux** (Eure, blvd. Georges-Chauvin, tel. 32–31–05–98), **Rouen** (Seine-Maritime, 2 bis rue du Petit-Salut, tel. 35–88–61–32), and **St-Lô** (Manche, rte. Villedieu, tel. 33–05–98–70).

Tourist offices of other major towns covered in this chapter are as follows: **Bayeux** (1 rue des Cuisiniers, tel. 31–92–16–26), **Dieppe** (1 blvd. du Général-de-Gaulle, tel. 35–84–11–77), **Fécamp** (pl. Bellet, tel. 35–28–20–51), **Le Havre** (1 pl. de l'Hôtel-de-Ville, tel. 35–21–22–88), and **Honfleur** (9 rue de la Ville, tel. 31–89–23–30).

Travel Agencies **American Express** (1–3 pl. Jacques-Lelieur, Rouen, tel. 35–98–19–80; 57 quai George V, Le Havre, tel. 35–42–59–11) and **Havas** (25 Grande-Rue, Alençon, tel. 33–32–88–88; 80 rue St-Jean, Caen, tel. 31–86–04–01; 14 pl. Nationale, Dieppe, tel. 35–84–29–16).

Car Rental	**Avis** (44 pl. de la Gare, Caen, tel. 31–87–31–84; 24 rue Malouet, Rouen, tel. 35–72–77–50) and **Europcar** (25 cours de la République, Le Havre, tel. 35–25–21–95).

Arriving and Departing

By Plane	Paris's Charles de Gaulle (Roissy) and Orly airports will be American visitors' closest link with the region. From the United Kingdom, there are regular flights to Caen and Deauville (from London) and to Cherbourg (from Southampton and the Channel Islands).
By Boat	Car ferries connect several Normandy ports with England and Ireland. There are crossings to Dieppe from Newhaven, to Le Havre from Portsmouth and Rosslare, and to Cherbourg from Portsmouth, Weymouth, and Rosslare.
By Car	The A13 expressway from Paris spears its way to Rouen in 1½ hours and to Caen in 2¼ hours. A13/N13 takes you to Cherbourg via Bayeux in another two hours.
By Train	From Paris's St-Lazare station, express trains stop at Rouen and Dieppe, Le Havre, or Fécamp, and at Caen and Cherbourg via Evreux and Lisieux. For Mont-St-Michel (nearest station: Pontorson), take the express from Paris's Montparnasse station to Rennes or to Caen (from St-Lazare) and switch to a local train.

Getting Around

By Plane	Normandy's domestic airports are at Rouen, Le Havre, and Evreux.
By Car	A13/N13 travels from Rouen to Cherbourg via Bayeux in two hours. Main roads also branch off from A13 to Le Havre (A15) and Dieppe (N27). To get to Mont-St-Michel, take A11 to Rennes, then N175 north.

Guided Tours

Bus and Car Excursions	**Viking Voyages** (16 rue du Général-Giraud, 14000 Caen, tel. 31–27–12–34) specializes in two-day packages by car, with overnight stays in private châteaus. Itineraries include "Normandy: From Rouen to Cherbourg"; "William the Conqueror's Route"; "Discovering the Manche," which includes a trip to Mont-St-Michel; a "D-Day Beaches" tour; and "From Lisieux to Suisse Normande." An all-inclusive tour, with car and English-speaking driver, is 1,850 francs. The **French Association of Travel Agents** offers a two-day tour of Mont-St-Michel and St-Malo, which includes a visit to Honfleur, the resorts of Deauville and Cabourg, the D-Day beaches, and Caen. The excursion, offered from April to October, costs 1,800 francs; contact **Clamageran Voyages** (4 rue Rollon, 76000 Rouen, tel. 35–07–39–07) for details.
Train Excursions	Both **Paris-Vision** (214 rue de Rivoli, 75001 Paris, tel. 42–60–31–25) and **Cityrama** (4 pl. des Pyramides, 75001 Paris, tel. 42–60–30–14) organize one-day train excursions to Mont-St-Michel, with a two-day option that takes in the châteaus of the Loire on the second day. Costing 800 francs, the one-day trips leave Paris at 7:15 PM on Saturday, arriving in Mont-St-Michel in time for lunch (included in the cost). Following a guided tour of

the mount and the abbey, you return to Paris—with a stop for dinner (also included in the cost) on the way—about 10:30 PM

Special-Interest **Viking Voyages** in Caen *(see above)* organizes bike trips around the region, as well as a "Normandy Antiques" tour by car. A two-day bike tour, without guide, costs 995 francs, while a guided antiques excursion costs 1,795 francs. **Trans Canal** in Caen (13 rond-point de l'Orne, tel. 31–34–00–00) arranges two-hour cruises on Caen's canal.

Personal Guides A number of cities organize their own tours, including Bayeux, Rouen, Caen, and Le Havre. For details, contact the individual tourist offices *(see* Tourist Information, *above).*

Exploring Normandy

Numbers in the margin correspond to points of interest on the Normandy map.

Orientation

We've divided our Norman coverage into three separate tours. The first tour leads northwest from Paris to Rouen, the capital of Upper Normandy. From here, we meander west to the port town of Le Havre before heading up along the impressive coastline of chalky cliffs and pebble beaches known as the Alabaster Coast.

Lower Normandy covers a much larger area, and we explore its sights in two itineraries. The first starts in the market town of Lisieux before heading north to the coastal resort of Honfleur, then west through the region's swankiest resort towns along the Calvados Coast. From here, we turn inland, to Caen and Bayeux. This area saw some of the fiercest fighting after the D-Day landings, as many monuments and memorials testify. The last stop is at the fabled Mont-St-Michel, which lies at the western edge of Normandy.

Finally, there's a scenic drive along the River Orne south of Caen, through the hilly region called La Suisse Normande.

Highlights for First-time Visitors

Abbaye aux Hommes, Caen, Tour 2
Bayeux Tapestry, Bayeux, Tour 2
Cliffs, Etretat, Tour 1
D-Day landing beaches, Tour 2
Deauville/Trouville, Tour 2
Honfleur, Tour 2
Musée des Beaux-Arts, Le Havre, Tour 1
Mont-St-Michel, Tour 2
Old Town, Rouen, Tour 1
View of La Suisse Normande from Roche d'Oëtre, Tour 3

Tour 1: Upper Normandy

Setting out from Paris, take the A13 expressway and branch off left, just after Bonnières-sur-Seine, to **Evreux**, capital of the Eure *département*. From the 5th century on, the town was ravaged and burnt by a succession of armies—first the Vandals, then the Normans, the English, and various French kings.

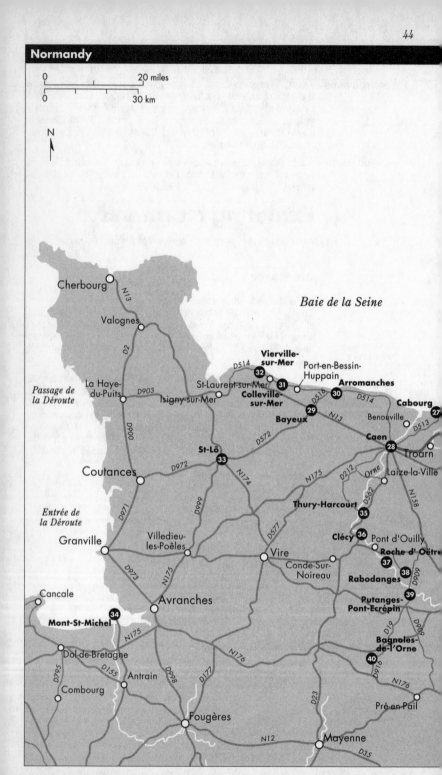

Normandy

0   20 miles

0   30 km

N

Cherbourg

N13

Valognes

Baie de la Seine

D2

*Passage de
la Déroute*

La Haye-
du-Puits

D903

D900

**Vierville-
sur-Mer**

D514

32

St-Laurent-sur-Mer

31

Port-en-Bessin-
Huppain

Arromanches

Isigny-sur-Mer

**Colleville-
sur-Mer**

D516

30

D514

Cabourg

27

29

N13

Benouville

D513

Bayeux

Caen

28

Troarn

D572

St-Lô

33

D972

N174

Coutances

Laize-la-Ville

D212

Orne

N158

N175

D562

D971

D999

D577

Thury-Harcourt

35

*Entrée de
la Déroute*

Granville

Villedieu-
les-Poêles

Vire

Clécy

36

Pont d'Ouilly

Roche d' Oëtre

37

D973

N175

Conde-Sur-
Noireau

38

D909

Rabodanges

39

Cancale

Avranches

**Putanges-
Pont-Ecrépin**

D19

D909

Mont-St-Michel

34

N175

**Bagnoles-
de-l'Orne**

Dol-de-Bretagne

D155

40

D916

N176

D795

Antrain

D998

D177

N176

Combourg

D23

Pré-en-Pail

Fougères

N12

Mayenne

D35

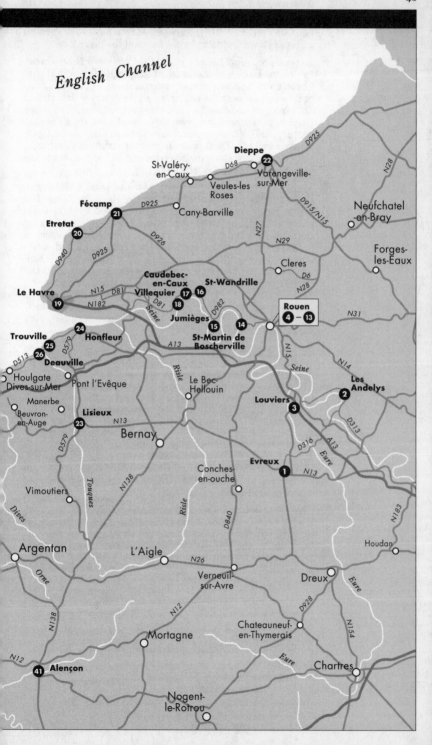

English Channel

Dieppe **22**
St-Valéry-
en-Caux
Veules-les
Roses
Varengeville-
sur-Mer
D68
D925
Neufchatel
-en-Bray
N28
D925/N15
Fécamp **21**
D925
Cany-Barville
Etretat **20**
N27
N29
Cleres
Forges-
les-Eaux
D940
D925
D926
D6
Caudebec-
en-Caux
St-Wandrille
N28
Le Havre **19**
N15 D81
Villequier
17 **16**
18
D982
Seine
N182
D81
Jumièges **15**
14
Rouen **4** — **13**
N31
Trouville
24 Honfleur
St-Martin de
Boscherville
A13
N15
Seine
N14
25
D579
26
Deauville
Risle
Le Bec-
Hellouin
Les
Andelys **2**
D513
Houlgate
Dives-sur-Mer
Pont l'Evêque
Louviers
3
D313
Manerbe
Beuvron-
en-Auge
Lisieux **23**
N13
Bernay
Conches-
en-ouche
Evreux **1**
N13
D316
A13
Eure
D579
Vimoutiers
Tougues
N138
Risle
D840
N183
Dives
L'Aigle
N26
Verneuil-
sur-Avre
Dreux
Eure
Houdan
Argentan
Orne
N138
N12
D928
N154
Chateauneuf-
en-Thymerais
Eure
Mortagne
N12
Alençon **41**
Chartres
Nogent-
le-Rotrou

World War II played its part as well. These days, the town has been well restored and is embellished by a number of gardens and overgrown footpaths by the banks of the River Iton.

Evreux's principal historic site is the **Cathédrale Notre-Dame,** (pl. Notre-Dame), in the heart of town just off rue Corbeau. Unfortunately, it was an easy victim of the many fires and raids that took place over the centuries; all that's left of the original 12th-century construction are the nave arcades. The lower parts of the chancel date from 1260, the chapels from the 14th century. Still, it's an outstanding example of Flamboyant Gothic inside and out. Don't miss the choir triforium and transept, the 14th-century stained-glass windows in the apse, or the entrance to the fourth chapel.

② From Evreux, get on D316 heading for **Les Andelys,** 36 kilometers (21 miles) away on the north bank of the River Seine. The pretty little town is set against magnificent chalky cliffs in one of the most picturesque loops of the River Seine. Overlooking the town from the clifftops and affording spectacular views in both directions are the remains of the **Château Gaillard,** a formidable fortress built by English king Richard the Lionhearted in 1196. Despite its solid defenses, the castle fell to the French in 1204. It had suffered considerable damage during the assault, and sections were later torn down at the end of the 16th century; only one of its five main towers remains intact. *Admission: 15 frs. Open Thurs.–Mon. 10–noon and 2–5, Wed. 2–5; closed Tues.*

Rather than take the most direct road from Les Andelys to Rouen (D126/D138), continue along D313 around the Seine for about 14 kilometers (9 miles), crossing it at St-Pierre du **③** Vauvry. You can then either stop at the busy town of **Louviers** on the Eure River to see its old houses and its Notre-Dame church or turn straight onto N15, the main road that passes just north of the town. Eight kilometers (5 miles) from Louviers, you'll cross the Pont de l'Arche, where the Eure and Seine rivers merge; from here, it's another 18 kilometers (11 miles) to Rouen. On the way, you'll pass through **Bonsecours,** now a suburb of the town and the site of the Basilique Notre-Dame, built in the early 1840s and one of the finest neo-Gothic churches in France.

④ The city of **Rouen** is a blend of ancient and modern, a large part having been destroyed during World War II. Even before its massive postwar reconstruction, the city had expanded outward during the 20th century with the development of industries spawned by its increasingly busy port, now the fifth largest in France. In its more distant past, Rouen gained celebrity when Joan of Arc was burned at the stake here in 1431.

Numbers in the margin correspond to points of interest on the Rouen map.

Rouen is known as the City of a Hundred Spires, and many of its important edifices are churches. Lording it over them all, in **⑤** place du Cathédrale, is the magnificent **Cathédrale Notre-Dame,** one of the masterpieces of French Gothic architecture. If you are familiar with the works of Impressionist Claude Monet, you will immediately recognize the cathedral's immense west facade, rendered in an increasingly misty, yet always beautiful, fashion in his series "Cathédrales de Rouen." The original 12th-century construction was replaced after a terri-

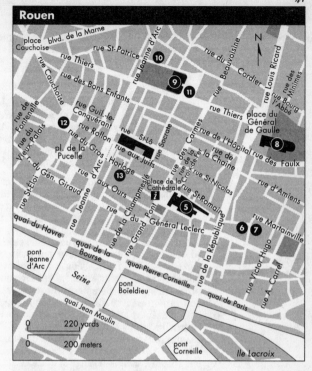

ble fire in 1200; only the left-hand spire, the Tour St-Romain,
survived the flames. The imposing 250-foot iron steeple on the
right, known as the "Butter Tower," was added in the 15th and
16th centuries and completed in the 17th, when a group of
wealthy citizens donated large sums of money—for the privilege of eating butter during Lent.

Interior highlights include the 13th-century choir, with its
pointed arcades; vibrant stained glass depicting the crucified
Christ (restored after heavy damage during World War II); and
massive stone columns topped by some intriguing carved faces.
The first flight of the famous Escalier de la Librairie (Booksell-
ers' Staircase) rises from a tiny balcony just to the left of the
transept and is attributed to Guillaume Pontifs, who is also responsible for most of the 15th-century work seen in the cathedral. *Pl. de la Cathédrale.*

Leaving the cathedral, head right, and cross rue de la République to place St-Maclou, an attractive square surrounded by picturesque half-timbered houses with steeply pointed roofs. The
❻ square's late-Gothic **Eglise St-Maclou** bears testimony to the
wild excesses of Flamboyant architecture; take time to exam-
ine the central and left-hand portals under the porchway on the
main facade, covered with little bronze lion heads and pagan
engravings. Inside, note the 16th-century organ, with its Renaissance wood carving, and the fine marble columns. *Pl. St-
Maclou.*

❼ To the right is the **Aître St-Maclou,** (184–186 rue Martainville),
a former ossuary that is one of the last reminders of the plague

that devastated Europe during the Middle Ages; these days, it holds Rouen's School of Art and Architecture. The ossuary (a charnel house used for the bodies of plague victims) is said to have inspired the French composer Camille Saint-Saëns (1835–1921) when he was working on his *Danse Macabre.* The building's massive double frieze is especially riveting, carved with some graphic skulls, bones, and gravediggers' tools.

❽ Turn right up rue de la République to place du Général-de-Gaulle, site of the **Eglise St-Ouen,** a fine example of late Gothic architecture. The stained-glass windows, dating from the 14th to the 16th centuries, are the most spectacular features of the otherwise spare structure. The church's 19th-century pipe organs have few equals in France.

❾ Walk west on rue Thiers to get to a cluster of Rouen's fine museums, the most important of which is the **Musée des Beaux-Arts** (Fine Arts Museum), on square Verdrel. It contains a fine collection of French paintings from the 17th and 19th centuries, including works by Claude Monet, Alfred Sisley, and Auguste Renoir. An entire room is devoted to Rouen-born Théodore Gericault, and there are impressive works by Delacroix and Chassériau. The museum once showcased a superb collection of Norman ceramics, but these are now housed separately ❿ in the **Musée de la Céramique** (Ceramic Museum), a few steps down the road (rue Faucon). A single ticket will get you into ⓫ both museums and into the **Musée de Ferronerie Le Secq des Tournelles,** right behind the Musée des Beaux-Arts. This museum claims to possess the world's finest collection of wrought iron, with exhibits spanning the 3rd through the 19th centuries. Displays include a range of items used in daily life, accessories, and professional instruments used by surgeons, barbers, carpenters, clockmakers, and gardeners. *Admission: 15 frs. All three museums are open Thurs.–Mon. 10–noon and 2–6, Wed. 2–6; closed Tues.*

⓬ Continue down rue Thiers, then turn left onto rue Jeanne-d'Arc and head toward place du Vieux-Marché, dominated by the thoroughly modern **Eglise Jeanne d'Arc.** Dedicated to the saint, the church was built on the spot where she was burned to death in 1431. Not all is spanking new, however; the church is graced with some remarkable 16th-century glass windows taken from the former Eglise St-Vincent, destroyed in 1944.

⓭ Leading out of place du Vieux-Marché is Rouen's most popular attraction, the rue du Gros-Horloge. The name of this little pedestrian street comes from the **Gros-Horloge** itself, a giant Renaissance clock; in 1527, the Rouennais had a splendid arch built especially for it, and today its golden face looks out over the street (the ticket to the Musée des Beaux-Arts includes admission to the ornate belfry). Though the ancient thoroughfare is crammed with boutiques and fast-food joints, a few old houses, dating from the 16th century, remain. Wander through the surrounding old town, a warren of tiny streets lined with over 700 half-timbered houses. Instead of standing simply as monuments to the past, these cobbled streets have been successfully transformed into a lively pedestrian shopping precinct, and the old buildings now contain the most fashionable shops in the city.

Numbers in the margin correspond to points of interest on the Normandy map.

The Seine Valley between Rouen and Le Havre is full of interesting sights, old and new, dotted amid some lovely scenery.
Within 10 minutes of Rouen, along D982, is the 11th-century
⑭ abbey church of St-George in **St-Martin de Boscherville**. From
here, follow D982 and D65 around the Seine for some 19 kilome-
⑮ ters (12 miles) to **Jumièges** to see the imposing ruins of its once-
mighty Benedictine abbey, the **Abbaye de Jumièges**, founded in
the 7th century and subsequently plundered by Vikings. The
abbey was rebuilt in the 11th century and consecrated in 1067,
but monks lived there until the French Revolution. It was then
auctioned off to a timber merchant, who promptly demolished a
large part of the building to sell the stones. *Tel. 35–37–24–02.
Admission: 24 frs. Open daily 10–noon and 2–6 (until 4 in winter).*

About 16 kilometers (10 miles) farther along the right bank of
⑯ the Seine, in **St.-Wandrille**, is another Benedictine abbey. The
Abbaye de St-Wandrille survives as an active monastery to this
day; like Jumièges, it was founded in the 7th century, sacked
(by the Normans), and rebuilt in the 10th century. You can still
hear the monks sing their Gregorian chants at morning Mass if
you're there early in the day (9:25 weekdays and 10 Sunday and
holidays). *Tel. 35–96–23–11. Guided tour at 3 and 4 weekdays;
cost: 18 frs. adults, children free.*

From St-Wandrille, it's only a couple of miles to the charming
⑰ little village of **Caudebec-en-Caux**; if the day is sunny, you
should leave the car and walk along the banks of the Seine. The
village's 15th-century Eglise Notre-Dame was described by
French monarch Henri IV (1589–1610) as "the most beautiful
chapel in the kingdom." A huge modern bridge, the Pont de
Brotonne, spans the Seine at Caudebec. Instead of crossing it,
however, drive west around the north bank of the Seine for a
⑱ couple of miles to **Villequier**, a peacefully situated riverside village dominated by its château. Villequier is famous as the place
where 19th-century writer Victor Hugo lost his daughter,
Léopoldine, and her husband, Charles Vacquerie, who
drowned in the Seine's notorious seasonal tidal wave (these
days it is held at bay by a dam). A museum, the **Musée Victor
Hugo**, has been created in the couple's old house; exhibits include the manuscript of Hugo's poem *Contemplations*, a la-
ment on their deaths. *Quai Victor-Hugo, tel. 35–56–78–31.
Admission: 10 frs. Open Wed.–Mon. 10–noon and 2–5:30,
closed Tues.*

Time Out If the weather's fine when you are in Villequier, stop off for a
light lunch at **Le Grand Sapin** (rue Louis-le-Graffic). The food is
plain, traditional fare, but the riverside terrace is delightful.

⑲ The seaside port of **Le Havre** lies 53 kilometers (33 miles) west
by D81 and N182. A bustling modern town, largely rebuilt after 1945, Le Havre is France's second-largest port (after Marseille). Le Havre was bombarded no fewer than 146 times
during World War II, and reinforced concrete and bleak open
spaces have not done much for the town's atmosphere. The old
seafaring quarter of Ste-Adresse is worth a visit, however.
From its fortress, you have panoramic views of the port and the
Seine estuary.

At the opposite end of the seafront, at the tip of boulevard
François-Ier, sits the metal-and-glass **Musée des Beaux-Arts**.

On the ground floor there's a remarkable collection of Raoul
Dufy's work, including oils, watercolors, and sketches. Dufy
(1877–1953) was born in Le Havre and devoted a lot of time to
his native region: views of Norman beaches and of Le Havre itself. If you can't spend much time in Normandy, go upstairs to
have a look at works by one of the forerunners of Impressionism—Eugène Boudin. Boudin's compelling beach scenes
and Norman countrysides will give you a taste of what you're
missing. *23 blvd. Clemenceau, tel. 35–42–33–97. Admission
free. Open Wed.–Mon. 10–noon and 2–6; closed Tues.*

The first stop on the coast between Le Havre and Dieppe (a
❷⓪ stretch known as the Alabaster Coast) is **Etretat**, about 30 kilometers (18 miles) away along D940. The town's white cliffs
are almost as famous in France as Dover's are in England. Although the promenade running the length of Etretat's pebble
beach has been spoiled by a proliferation of seedy cafés and
french-fry stands, the town retains its vivacity and charm. Its
landmarks are two arched cliff formations, the **Falaise d'Amont**
and the **Falaise d'Aval,** which jut out over the sea on either side
of the bay, and a 300-foot needle of rock, the **Aiguille,** which
thrusts up from the sea near the Falaise d'Amont. Through the
huge archways carved by the sea into the cliffs, you can walk to
neighboring beaches at low tide. For a breathtaking view of the
whole bay, take the path up to the Falaise d'Aval on the southern side, from which you can hike for miles across the Manne-
porte hills.

Seventeen kilometers (11 miles) from Etretat along D940 is
❷① **Fécamp,** an ancient fishing port that was Normandy's primary
place of pilgrimage before Mont-St-Michel stole all the glory.
Fécamp no longer has a commercial fishing fleet, but you will
still see lots of boats in the private yachting marina. The magnificent **Eglise La Trinité** (just off blvd. de la République) bears
witness to the town's religious past. The Benedictine abbey
was founded by the duke of Normandy in the 11th century and
became the home of the monastic order of the Précieux Sang et
de la Trinité (referring to Christ's blood, which supposedly ar-
rived here in the 7th century). Fécamp is also the home of the
liqueur Benedictine. The **Musée de la Bénédictine,** seven blocks
across town on rue Boufart, was rebuilt in 1892 in a florid mixture of neo-Gothic and Renaissance styles and remains one of
Normandy's most popular attractions. *110 rue Alexandre-le-
Grand, tel. 35–28–00–06. Admission: 25 frs. (including a tast-
ing). Open Easter–mid-Nov., daily 9:30–12 and 2–6.*

From Fécamp it's about 65 kilometers (40 miles) to Dieppe; take
D925 via Cany-Barville to St-Valéry-en-Caux and Veules-les-
Roses and then the scenic coast road, D68, the rest of the way.
Just before reaching Dieppe, you'll pass through **Varengeville-
sur-Mer.** Look for the tiny church perched on a hill: 20th-centu-
ry painter Georges Braque—who, with Picasso, is credited
with inventing Cubism—is buried in its graveyard. If you like
gardens, don't miss the **Parc des Moustiers,** with its rare flowers
and giant 100-year-old rhododendrons. *La Haie des Moustiers,
tel. 35–85–10–02. Admission: 35 frs. Open daily 10–noon and
2–6.*

❷② **Dieppe** is a charming blend of a fishing and commercial port and
a Norman seaside town. The boulevard du Maréchal-Foch, a
seafront promenade, separates an immense lawn from an unspoiled pebble beach where, in 1942, many Canadian soldiers

were killed during the so-called Jubilee raid. Overlooking the Channel, at the western end of the bay, stands the 15th-century **Château de Dieppe,** which dominates the town from its clifftop position. It contains the town museum, well known for its collection of ivories. In the 17th century, Dieppe imported vast quantities of elephant tusks from Africa and Asia, and as many as 350 craftsmen settled here to work the ivory; their efforts can be seen in the form of ship models, nautical accessories, or, upstairs, in religious and day-to-day objects. The museum also has a room devoted to sketches by Georges Braque. *Sq. du Canada, tel. 35–84–19–76. Admission: 12 frs. Open mid-Sept.–mid-June, Wed.–Mon. 10–noon and 2–5 (until 6 Sun.); closed Tues.*

Tour 2: The Calvados Coast and Mont-St-Michel

㉓ **Lisieux** is the main market town of the prosperous Pays d'Auge, an agricultural region famous for cheeses named after such towns as Camembert, Pont l'Evêque, and Livarot. It is also a land of apple orchards from which the finest Calvados brandy comes. Lisieux emerged relatively unscathed from World War II, though it boasts few historical monuments beyond the **Cathédrale St-Pierre,** built in the 12th and 13th centuries. It is also famous for its patron saint, Ste-Thérèse, who was born and died in the last quarter of the 19th century, having spent the last 10 of her 25 years as a Carmelite nun. Thérèse was canonized in 1925, and in 1954 a basilica—one of the world's largest 20th-century churches—was dedicated to her; to get there from the cathedral, walk up avenue Victor-Hugo and branch left into avenue Jean-XXIII.

㉔ From Lisieux, take D579 north to Pont l'Evêque and stay on that road when it forks right toward **Honfleur,** a distance of 32 kilometers (20 miles). This colorful port on the Seine estuary epitomizes Normandy for many people. It was once an important departure point for maritime expeditions, and the first voyages to Canada in the 15th and 16th centuries embarked from here. Its 17th-century harbor is fronted on one side by two-story stone houses with low, sloping roofs and on the other by tall, narrow houses whose wooden facades are topped by slate roofs. The whole town is a museum piece, full of half-timbered houses and cobbled streets.

Honfleur was colonized by French and foreign painters in the 19th century, and the group later known as the Impressionists used to meet in the **Ferme St-Siméon,** now a luxurious hotel (*see* Dining and Lodging, *below*). Honfleur has also inspired other artists: Charles Baudelaire, the 19th-century poet and champion of Romanticism, wrote his poem *L'Invitation au Voyage* here, and the French composer Erik Satie was born in Honfleur in 1866.

Today Honfleur is one of the most popular vacation spots in northern France. During the summer, its hotels rarely have vacancies and its cafés and restaurants are always packed. Soak up the seafaring atmosphere by strolling around the old harbor and pay a visit to the **Eglise Ste-Catherine,** which dominates the harbor's northern corner (rue des Logettes). The wooden church was built by townspeople to show their gratitude for the departure of the English at the end of the Hundred

Years' War (1453), when masons and architects were occupied with national reconstruction.

Leave Honfleur by D513 west and follow the coast for 14 kilometers (9 miles) until you arrive at the twin seaside resorts of **Trouville** and **Deauville**, separated only by the estuary of the River Touques. Although Trouville is now considered an overflow town for its more prestigious neighbor, it became one of France's first seaside resorts when Parisians began flocking here in the mid-19th century.

Deauville is a chic watering hole for the French bourgeoisie and would-be fashionable personalities from farther afield, who are attracted by its racecourse, casino, marina and regattas, palaces and gardens, and, of course, its sandy beach. The **Promenade des Planches**—the boardwalk extending along the seafront and lined with deck chairs, bars, and striped cabanas—is the place for celebrity spotting. Nevertheless, if you are looking for authenticity rather than glamour, stay in Trouville. It, too, has a casino and boardwalk as well as a bustling fishing port and a native population that makes it a livelier place out of season than Deauville.

Time Out   One of the most popular places in Trouville is **Les Vapeurs,** a friendly, animated brasserie with neon-lit '50s decor. It serves good, fresh food at any time, day or night, and both the famous and not-so-famous like to meet here after dark. *160 blvd. Fernand-Moureaux. Closed Tues. dinner and Wed.*

Continue west along D513, which takes you through a number of family seaside resorts, such as pretty Houlgate and nearby Dives-sur-Mer, before reaching the larger and more elegant resort of **Cabourg,** just across the River Dives. Cabourg's streets fan out from a central hub near the seafront where the casino and the Grand Hôtel are situated. The early 20th-century novelist Marcel Proust, author of *Remembrance of Things Past*, was a great admirer of the town's pleasant seaside atmosphere and spent much of his time here. One of the volumes in his epic paints a perfect picture of life in the resort, to which the town responded by naming its magnificent seafront promenade after him.

Leave Cabourg by D513, which veers inland and after 24 kilometers (15 miles) brings you to **Caen,** the capital of Lower Normandy. Caen, with its abbeys and castle, presents a strong contrast to the somewhat uniform coastal resorts.

William of Normandy ruled from Caen in the 11th century before he conquered England. Nine hundred years later, the two-month Battle of Caen devastated the town in 1944. Much of the city burned in a fire that raged for 11 days, and the downtown area was almost entirely rebuilt after the war.

A good place to begin exploring is at the town's main tourist attraction, the **Abbaye aux Hommes,** a monastery built by William the Conqueror. "The Men's Abbey" was begun in Romanesque style in 1066 and was added to during the 18th century. Note the magnificent facade of the abbey church, the Eglise St-Etienne, whose spareness is enhanced by two 11th-century towers topped by Norman Gothic octagonal spires. Inside, what had been William the Conqueror's tomb was destroyed by 16th-century Huguenots during the Wars of Religion, but the choir still stands; it was the first to be built in Norman Gothic style, and many subsequent choirs were modeled after it. *Pl. Louis-Guillouard, tel. 31–30–41–00. Guided tours of the abbey cost 10 frs. Open daily 9–noon and 2–5.*

Head right up Fosses St-Julien to the Esplanade du Château. The ruins of William the Conqueror's **fortress,** built in 1060 and sensitively restored after the war, glower down on all who approach. The castle gardens are a perfect spot for strolling, and the ramparts afford good views of the city. Within the rampart walls lies the **Musée des Beaux-Arts,** a Fine Arts Museum whose impressive collection includes Rembrandts and Titians. Also within the castle are the **Musée de Normandie,** displaying regional arts, and the chapel of St-George. *Entrance by the Porte sur la Ville, tel. 31–86–06–24. Admission to each: 6 frs. (free Sun.) Open Wed.–Mon. 9:30–12:30 and 2–6; closed Tues.*

Take rue des Chanoines right to the **Abbaye aux Dames,** the "Ladies' Abbey," built by William the Conqueror's wife, Matilda, in 1062. The abbey is now a hospital and not open to visitors, but you can visit its Église de la Trinité. This squat church is a good example of 11th-century Romanesque architecture, though its original spires were replaced by bulky balustrades in the early 18th century. The 11th-century crypt once held Matilda's tomb, which was destroyed during the French Revolution. Note the intricate carvings on columns and arches in the chapel. *Pl. Reine-Mathilde. Admission free. Guided tours daily at 2:30 and 4.*

Head back down the rue des Chanoines and continue on rue Montoir-Poissonnerie. Turning left onto place St-Pierre, you'll come face-to-face with the Caen Tourist Office. It merits a visit not only for its excellent information resources, but for its splendid site in the **Hôtel d'Escoville,** a 16th-century mansion built by a wealthy town merchant, Nicolas le Valois d'Escoville. The building was badly damaged during the war but has since been restored; the austere facade conceals an elaborate inner courtyard, reflecting the Italian influence on early Renaissance Norman architecture.

A good introduction to the Normandy landings of 1944 can be had at the **Mémorial,** a museum opened in the north of the city in 1988. Videos, photos, arms, paintings, and prints detail the Battle of Normandy and the French Liberation. *Esplanade Général-Eisenhower, tel. 31–06–06–44. Admission: 45 frs. adults, 19 frs. students. Open May–Sept., daily 9–6 (until 7 Sun.).*

㉙ From Caen, N13 heads 28 kilometers (17 miles) northwest to **Bayeux,** an attractive town steeped in history and the first town to be liberated during the Battle of Normandy. Bayeux's long history stretches back many centuries before World War II, however, and we begin our tour at the **Musée de la Tapisserie,** located in an 18th-century building on rue de Nesmond and showcasing the world's most celebrated piece of needlework, the **Bayeux Tapestry.** The medieval work of art—stitched in 1067—is really a 225-foot-long embroidered scroll, which depicts, in 58 separate scenes, the epic story of William of Normandy's conquest of England in 1066, a watershed in European history. The tapestry's origins remain obscure, though it was probably commissioned from Saxon embroiderers by the count of Kent—also the bishop of Bayeux—to be displayed in his newly built cathedral. Despite its age, the tapestry is in remarkably good condition; the extremely detailed, often homey scenes provide an unequaled record of the clothes, weapons, ships, and lifestyles of the day. *Centre Guillaume Le Conquérant, 13 bis, rue de Nesmond, tel. 31–92–05–48. Admission: 25 frs. (6 frs. for a cassette translation). Open June–Sept., daily 9–7; Oct.–May, daily 9:30–12:30 and 2–6.*

Your ticket also gains you entrance to the **Musée Baron Gérard**. Head up rue de Nesmond to rue Larchet, turning left into lovely place des Tribuneaux. The museum contains fine collections of Bayeux porcelain and lace, ceramics from Rouen, and 16th–19th-century furniture and paintings. *1 rue la Chaîne, tel. 31–92–14–21. Admission: 15 frs. adults, 10 frs. senior citizens. Open daily, June–Aug., 9–7; Sept.–mid-Oct. and Mar.–May, 9:30–12:30 and 2–6:30; mid-Oct.–Mar., 10–12:30 and 2–6.*

Behind the museum, with an entrance on rue de Bienvenu, sits Bayeux's most important historic building, the **Cathédrale Notre-Dame.** The cathedral is a harmonious mixture of Norman and Gothic architecture. Note the portal on the south side of the transept, which depicts the assassination of English Archbishop Thomas à Becket in Canterbury Cathedral in 1170, following his opposition to King Henry II's attempts to control the church.

Return to the 20th century by turning left, walking to the place au Blois, and continuing down rue St-Loup. Turn right on boulevard du Général-Fabian-Ware, site of the **Musée de la Bataille de Normandie,** whose detailed exhibits trace the story of the Battle of Normandy from June 7 to August 22, 1944. The ultramodern museum contains an impressive array of war paraphernalia, including uniforms, weapons, and equipment. *Blvd. Général-Fabian-Ware, tel. 31–92–45–55. Admission: 20 frs. Open June–Aug., daily 9–7; Sept.–Oct. and Mar.–May, daily 10–12:30 and 2–6:30; and Nov.–Feb., weekends 10:30–12:30 and 2–6:30.*

Operation Overlord, the code name for the Invasion of Normandy, called for five beachheads—dubbed Utah, Omaha, Gold, Juno, and Sword—to be established along the Calvados Coast, to either side of Arromanches. Preparations started in mid-1943, and British shipyards worked furiously through the following winter and spring building two artificial harbors (called Mulberries), boats, and landing equipment. The operation was originally scheduled to take place on June 5, but poor weather caused it to be postponed for a day.

The British troops that landed on Sword, Juno, and Gold quickly pushed inland and joined with parachute regiments that had been dropped behind the German lines. U.S. forces met with far tougher opposition on Omaha and Utah beaches, however, and it took them six days to secure their positions and meet the other Allied forces. From there, they pushed south and west, cutting off the Cotentin Peninsula on June 10 and taking Cherbourg on June 26. Meanwhile, British forces were encountering fierce resistance at Caen and did not take it until July 9. By then, U.S. forces were turning their attention southward, but it took two weeks of bitter fighting to dislodge the Germans from the area around St-Lô; the town was finally liberated on July 19.

After having boned up on the full story of the Normandy invasion, you'll want to go and see the area where it all took place. There's little point in visiting all five sites, since not much remains to mark the furious fighting waged hereabouts. In the bay of Arromanches, however, some elements of the floating harbor are still visible.

30 Head north from Bayeux along D516 to **Arromanches,** 10 kilometers (6 miles) away. Linger here a while, contemplating those seemingly insignificant hunks of concrete protruding from the water, and try to imagine the extraordinary technical feat involved in towing the two floating harbors across the Channel from England. (The other was moored at Omaha Beach but was destroyed on June 19, 1944, by an exceptionally violent storm.) If you're interested in yet more battle documentation, visit the **Musée du Débarquement,** right on the seafront, whose exhibits include models, mock-ups, and photographs depicting the invasion. *Pl. du 6-Juin, tel. 31–22–34–31. Admission: 15 frs. adults, 10 frs. students. Open July and Aug., daily 9–7; Sept.– June, 9–11:30 and 2–5:30.*

From Arromanches, take D514 west.

Time Out About 10 kilometers (6 miles) along, you'll reach Port-en-Bessin-Huppain, a little fishing port that has a striking restaurant called **La Marine** (quai Letourneur). The fish and seafood are fresh, and the upstairs dining room offers terrific views of the port.

Continue along D514 for another 8 kilometers (5 miles) to **31** **Colleville-sur-Mer,** then turn right to **Omaha Beach,** scene of a bloody battle in which nearly 10,000 American soldiers lost their lives. A little farther along D514, at St-Laurent-sur-Mer, turn right onto D517, which takes you back to the seafront at the site of the **Monument du Débarquement** (Monument to the Normandy Landings). You may want to park the car and stroll around the beaches and the grassy tops of the dunes overlooking them, from which you'll see sad remnants of the war—ruined bunkers, rows of trenches, and the remains of barbed-wire **32** defenses. Continue along the beachfront to **Vierville-sur-Mer,** which has a monument to the members of the U.S. National Guard who fought in both world wars.

Unless you decide to drive into the Cotentin Peninsula, past Utah Beach and on to Cherbourg, you can conclude your tour of the Calvados Coast either by returning to Bayeux via Isigny-sur-Mer, about 19 kilometers (12 miles) from Vierville, or by **33** continuing to St-Lô, 29 kilometers (18 miles) from Isigny. Given its sad sobriquet of the "capital of ruins," you won't be surprised that St-Lô played a strategic role in the Battle of Normandy and was almost completely destroyed in July 1944. The town was largely rebuilt after the war, and its only relic of the past is the ruined 13th–17th-century Eglise Notre-Dame.

If you're interested in cathedral architecture, you'll want to make a trip to **Coutances,** 29 kilometers (18 miles) west of St-Lô along D972. Many consider the largely 13th-century Cathédrale Notre-Dame, with its famous octagonal lantern rising 41 meters (135 feet) above the nave, to be the most harmonious and impressive Gothic building in Normandy.

Otherwise, take D999 from St-Lô, which joins with N175 at Villedieu-les-Poêles, and continue to Avranches; from here, follow the road around the bay to the Abbey of **Mont-St-Michel.** Before you visit this awe-inspiring monument, be warned that the sea that separates the rock from the mainland is extremely dangerous: It's subject to tidal movements that produce a difference of up to 45 feet between low and high tides, and because of the extremely flat bay bed, the water rushes in at an incredible speed. Also, there are nasty patches of quicksand, so tread with care!

The dramatic silhouette of Mont-St-Michel against the horizon may well be your most lasting image of Normandy. The wonder of the abbey stems not only from its rocky perch a few hundred yards off the coast (it's cut off from the mainland at high tide), but from its legendary origins in the 8th century and the sheer exploit of its construction, which took more than 500 years, from 1017 to 1521. The abbey stands at the top of a 264-foot mound of rock, and the granite used to build it was transported from the Isles of Chausey (just beyond Mont-St-Michel Bay) and Brittany and laboriously hauled up to the site.

Legend has it that the Archangel Michael appeared to Aubert, bishop of Avranches, inspiring him to build an oratory on what was then called Mont Tombe. The original church was completed in 1144, but new buildings were added in the 13th century to accommodate the monks, as well as the hordes of pilgrims who flocked here even during the Hundred Years' War, when the region was in English hands. The Romanesque choir was rebuilt in an ornate Gothic style during the 15th and 16th centuries. The abbey's monastic vocation was undermined during the 17th century, when the monks began to flout the strict rules and discipline of their order, a drift into decadence that culminated in the monks' dispersal and the abbey's conversion into a prison well before the French Revolution. In 1874, the former abbey was handed over to a governmental agency responsible for the preservation of historical monuments; only within the past 20 years have monks been able to live and work here once more.

A highlight of the abbey is the collection of 13th-century buildings on the north side of the mount. The exterior of the buildings is grimly fortresslike, but inside they are one of Normandy's best examples of the evolution of Gothic architecture, ranging from the sober Romanesque style of the lower halls to the masterly refinement of the cloisters and the elegance of the refectory.

A causeway—soon to be replaced by a bridge, thus allowing the bay waters to circulate freely—links Mont-St-Michel to the mainland. Leave your car in the parking lot at the foot of the mount, outside the main gateway.

The climb to the abbey is hard going, but it's worth it. Head first for the Grand Degré, the steep, narrow staircase on the north side. Once past the ramparts, you'll come to the pink-and-gray granite towers of the Châtelet and then to the Salle des Gardes, the central point of the abbey. Guided tours start from the Saut Gautier terrace (named after a prisoner who jumped to his death from it): You must join one of these groups if you want to see the beautifully wrought Escalier de Dentelle (Lace Staircase) inside the church. *Admission: 35 frs. Open mid-May–Sept., daily 9:30–11:30 and 1:30–6; Oct.–mid-May, Wed.–Mon. 9–11 and 1:30–4, closed Tues.*

The island village, with its steep, narrow streets, is best visited out of season, from September to May. The hordes of souvenir sellers and tourists can be stifling in summer months, but you can always take refuge in the abbey's gardens. The ramparts in general and the North Tower in particular offer dramatic views of the bay.

Tour 3: La Suisse Normande

Caen is the best starting point for a trip through La Suisse Normande, or Swiss Normandy, a rocky expanse of hills and gullies in the heart of Lower Normandy, containing lots of natural beauty and few man-made wonders. Striking as the scenery is, however, you'll need to exert all your powers of imagination to see much resemblance to the Swiss Alps! Taking D562 south for 45 kilometers (28 miles), you'll come to 35 **Thury-Harcourt** on the Orne River, the gateway to La Suisse Normande. If you're not in a hurry and you enjoy twisting country roads, turn right off D562 at Laize-la-Ville, cross the Orne, and take the more scenic D212, which runs alongside the river and enters Thury-Harcourt from the opposite bank. This little country town is famous for the beautiful gardens of its ruined castle.

36 Continue down D562, following the Orne, to **Clécy**, the area's main tourist center. It's a good base for visiting the sights of the Orne Valley; take the steep roads up to the clifftops overlooking the river, where there are lovely views of the woods on the other bank.

Time Out You'll find an open-air, riverbank café in Clécy, **La Potinière**, which is great for drinks or snacks. Crepes top the bill, either sweet or with savory fillings such as ham and cheese, and there's a good selection of tarts and homemade ice cream. On Friday evening, you can enjoy a rowdy musical backdrop of jazz or rock. *On the river. Closed Oct.–Apr.*

From Clécy, continue for a couple of miles along D562 and then turn left at Le Fresne onto D1, which winds its way through the valley of the Noireau to another riverside resort, Pont d'Ouilly, situated at the point where the River Noireau flows into the Orne. Heading south along the Orne on D167, veer right at le Pont-des-Vers onto D43 and head into the most 37 mountainous part of La Suisse Normande to the **Roche d'Oëtre**; from here, you'll get the most spectacular views of the craggy hills that give the region its name.

Continue along D301 for a few miles and then turn left across the Orne, joining D21 before turning almost immediately right 38 along D239 to **Rabodanges**. Turn down any of the side roads leading to the riverside, where you'll be rewarded with a fine view of the river gorge (the Gorges de St-Aubert). A little farther upstream is the Rabodanges dam; from here, D121 skirts the eastern side of the lake. The road crosses the lake by the 39 Ste-Croix bridge and takes you to **Putanges-Pont-Ecrépin**.

The Orne River now swings east to Argentan, a peaceful little town that was badly damaged during the last days of the Battle of Normandy. Rather than follow the river, however, it's more

rewarding to head south from Putanges, along D909 and then
D19, to **Bagnoles-de-l'Orne**, the most important spa town in the
region. The town nestles in a beautiful setting overlooking a
lake formed by the River Yée and is surrounded by forests and
parkland that are well worth touring.

From Bagnoles-de-l'Orne, it's a fairly straight road to **Alençon**;
follow D916 south, then turn left onto N176 to Pré-en-Pail and
take N12 from there. The road runs through the middle of the
Normandie-Maine Nature Park. Alençon lies on the eastern
edge of the park, south of the Forest of Ecouves and west of the
Forest of Perseigne. An attractive town with many historic
buildings, Alençon has been a lace-making center since 1665;
by the end of the 17th century Alençon lace was de rigueur in
all fashionable circles. The **Musée des Beaux-Arts et de la
Dentelle** contains a sophisticated collection of lace from Italy,
Flanders, and France, along with paintings from the French
school that span the 17th to the 20th centuries. *Rue Charles-
Aveline, tel. 33–32–40–07. Admission: 12 frs. Open Tues.–
Sun. 10–noon and 2–6.*

Turn right out of the museum and head right again at the corner. Seven blocks down, you'll come to the 14th–15th-century
Eglise Notre-Dame (rue St-Blaize), erected around 1500 and
known for its highly ornate Gothic porch.

What to See and Do with Children

The **Parc Zoologique de Clères**, 16 kilometers (10 miles) north of
Rouen, is a wildlife park that's home to more than 750 species of
birds, plus a motley assortment of free-roaming antelope,
deer, kangaroos, and gibbons. Clères is a tiny village; you can't
miss the park. *Tel. 35–33–23–08. Admission: 25 frs. adults, 15
frs. children under 15. Open Mar.–May and Sept.–Nov., daily
9–noon and 3:30–sunset; June–Aug., daily 9–sunset.*

A **vintage-car museum** is found at Le Bec-Hellouin, southwest
of Rouen. Even those who are long past childhood will appreci-
ate the 50 racing and touring automobiles from as early as 1920;
the highlights must be the seven Bugattis. *Tel. 32–44–86–06.
Admission: 25 frs. Open 9–noon and 2–7; closed Wed. and
Thurs. in winter.*

Most Norman resort beaches have supervised play areas where
children can happily spend a half day or so with their peers.

Off the Beaten Track

Connoisseurs of the apple brandy Calvados will be interested
in a visit to the **Vallée d'Auge,** on the west side of the Pays
d'Auge. This is the heart of Calvados country, between Troarn
and Lisieux, through which the River Dives and its tributaries
flow. You don't need a fixed itinerary; just follow your nose and
look for local farmers offering Calvados for sale. However,
there is a pretty, winding route to follow from Manerbe, north
of Lisieux, which meanders west along D270, D117, and D85 to
Beuvron-en-Auge, where you take D117 again across the River
Dives to Troarn. Local Calvados producers will be delighted to
let you taste their products, especially if you then buy a few
bottles. They use traditional methods to distill the brandy, so
you can be sure of finding something superior to the brands
available in most shops.

Northwest of Evreux is **Le Bec-Hellouin,** near Brionne. Its famous Abbaye du Bec-Hellouin dates from the 11th century, but
the monks were driven out during the French Revolution and
the original abbey was demolished during the 19th century.
Only the 15th-century St-Nicolas tower, part of the south transept, and the bases of some pillars remain, together with a
13th-century Gothic door and some statues from the 14th and
15th centuries. Next to the abbey is a vintage car museum *(see*
What to See and Do with Children, *above). Abbaye du Bec-
Hellouin, tel. 32-44-86-09. Admission: 18 frs. Guided tours
only, Wed.–Mon. June–Sept. at 10, 11, 3, 3:45, 4:30, and 5:15;
Oct.–May at 11, 3:15, and 4:30.*

Shopping

Lace
Handmade lace is a great rarity, and admirers will certainly
think it's worth spending some time searching it out. Prices are
high, but then, this kind of labor-intensive, high-quality creation never comes cheap. In Alençon, try the **Musée de la
Dentelle** (31 rue du Pont-Neuf). In Bayeux, try the **Centre
Normand de la Dentelle** on rue Leforestier.

Food Items
Normandy is a food-lover's region, and some of the best buying
is to be done in food markets and charcuteries. Gastronomes
will want to drop by **La Ferme Normande** (13 rue Breney, Deauville) for regional delicacies, while those with a weakness for
sweets should go straight to **Raten** (115 Grande-Rue, Dieppe).

Spirits
It's true that you can buy Benedictine anywhere in the world,
but if you've visited the **Musée de la Bénédictine** (110 rue
Alexandre-le-Grand) in Fécamp, the bottle you buy there will
have a certain sentimental value. Calvados is harder to find
outside France, and although it's generally available in wine
shops around the country, you'll find a wider choice of good-
quality Calvados in Normandy itself. If possible, buy Calvados
that comes from the Vallée d'Auge, the area of Normandy re-
puted to produce the best *(see* Off the Beaten Track, *above).* In
Dives, the **Cave du Bois Hibout** (2 pl. de la République) offers
first-rate Calvados.

Antiques Fairs
and Markets
If you enjoy the hunt as much as the prize, try the following:
Caen hosts a bric-a-brac and antiques fair in June, while
Cabourg has one in mid-August. Caen also has two morning
flea markets: on Sunday in place Courtonne and on Friday in
place St-Saveur.

Beaches

Wherever you go on the Normandy Coast, you'll look at the chil-
ly waters of the English Channel: Those used to warmer climes
may need all their resolve to take the plunge, even on hot, sunny days. The most fashionable Norman resorts lie along the
Floral Coast, the eastern end of the Calvados Coast between
Deauville/Trouville and Cabourg; it's virtually one long, sandy
beach, with the different towns overlapping. The rest of the
Calvados Coast is also a succession of seaside resorts, though
the beaches that saw the Normandy landings have not been so
developed as those farther east. While the resort towns of the
western Calvados Coast don't lack for charm, they don't have
the character of Honfleur or the unspoiled and rugged beauty

of the pebbly Alabaster Coast, stretching from Le Havre to beyond Dieppe. The resorts here are more widely spaced, separated by craggy cliffs, and even in the summer months, beaches are relatively uncrowded. Perched on the clifftops are green fields and woodland where you can amble for hours, breathing the fresh sea air.

Sports and Fitness

Biking You can rent bicycles from train stations in Bayeux, Caen, Dieppe, and Le Tréport for about 40 francs per day. Or try **Family Home** in Bayeux (39 rue du Gal-Dais, tel. 31–92–15–22).

Golf The most spectacular golf course in Normandy is at **Le Vaudrueil,** in a park that nestles between two branches of the River Eure; the course takes you past the ruins of a number of old castles. Other 18-hole courses are found in Cabourg, Deauville, Etretat, Dieppe, Le Havre, and Rouen, and there are nine-hole courses in Deauville, Houlgate, and Bagnoles-de-l'Orne.

Hiking There are 10 long-distance, signposted itineraries and countless well-indicated footpaths for shorter walks; overnight hostels are found at many points. Contact the **Comité Départemental de la Randonnée Pedestre de Seine-Maritime** (B.P. 666, 76008 Rouen).

Horseback Riding Normandy is a leading horseracing and training region, with numerous stud farms, Thoroughbred stables, and racecourses. The most important race of the year is the Grand Prix at Deauville, on the last Sunday in August. If you prefer riding to watching, contact Upper Normandy's center for equestrian tourism, the **Association Régionale de Tourisme Equestre** in Caen (Chambre d'Agriculture, 4 promenade Mme-de-Sévigné, 14039 Caen, tel. 31–84–47–19).

Rock Climbing There is good rock-climbing country in the Seine Valley and in the region of La Suisse Normande; inquire at **C.A.F.** (13 rue Jacques-Durandes, 14000 Caen, tel. 31–93–07–23).

Water Sports With its miles of coastline, its rivers, and its lakes, Normandy offers a multitude of water-based activities. Many resorts have yachting marinas, where you can rent sailing dinghies and windsurfers as well as water-ski. At the **Deauville Yacht Club** (quai de la Marine, tel. 31–88–38–19), a day in the smallest boat (16 feet) costs just 80 francs, while an 80-foot yacht will set you back about 500 francs. Similar prices are encountered at **Le Club Nautique de Trouville** (Digue des Roches Noires, tel. 31–88–13–59). For swimmers, there are 60 outdoor and 20 indoor pools, in addition to the many safe bathing beaches; you can find public swimming pools in Bayeux, Cabourg, Caen, Deauville, Trouville, and Lisieux. The charming resort of Granville, 26 kilometers (16 miles) northwest of Avranches, is a center for aquatic sports; inquire about sailboat jaunts at the **Centre Regional de Nautisme de Granville** (Anse de Hérel, 50400 Granville, tel. 33–50–18–95). **Lepesqueux Voile** (3 rue Clément-Desmaisons, 50400 Granville, tel. 33–50–18–97) rents boats and yachts for vacation cruises.

Dining and Lodging

Dining

Normandy is the land of butter, cream cheese, and Calvados. The Normans are notoriously big eaters: In the old days, on festive occasions they wouldn't bat an eye at tucking into as many as 24 courses. Between the warm-up and the main course there was a *trou* (hole), often lasting several hours, during which lots of Calvados was downed, giving rise to the expression *le trou normand*.

Many dishes are cooked with rich cream sauces; the description *à la normande* usually means "with a cream sauce." The richness of the milk makes for excellent cheese: Pont-l'Évêque (known since the 13th century) is made in the Pays d'Auge with milk that is still warm and creamy, while Livarot (also produced for centuries) uses milk that has stood for a while; don't be put off by its strong smell. Then there are the excellent Pavé d'Auge and the best known of them all, Camembert, a relative newcomer, invented by a farmer's wife in the late 18th century. Now so popular that it is produced all over France, the best Camembert is still made in Normandy (known as *Camembert au lait cru*).

There are many local specialties. Rouen is famous for its *canard à la Rouennaise* (duck in blood sauce); Caen, for its *tripes à la mode de Caen* (tripe cooked with carrots in a seasoned cider stock); and Mont-St-Michel, for *omelette Mère Poulard* (a hearty omelette made by a local hotel manager in the late 19th century for travelers to Mont-St-Michel). Then there are *sole dieppoise* (sole poached in a sauce with cream and mussels), excellent chicken from the Vallée d'Auge, and lamb from the salt marshes. Those who like *boudin noir* (blood sausage) have come to the right region, and for seafood lovers, the coast provides oysters, lobster, and shrimp.

Normandy is not a wine-growing area, but it produces excellent cider. The best comes from the Vallée d'Auge and is 100% apple juice; when poured into the glass, it should fizz a bit without frothing.

Highly recommended restaurants are indicated by a star ★.

Category	Cost*
Very Expensive	over 400 francs
Expensive	250–400 francs
Moderate	125–250 francs
Inexpensive	under 125 francs

*per person for a three-course meal, including tax (18.6%) and tip but not wine

Lodging

There are accommodations to suit every taste in Normandy. In the beach resorts, the season is very short, July and August only, but weekends are busy for much of the year; in June and

September, accommodations are usually available at short notice.

Highly recommended hotels are indicated by a star ★.

Category	Cost*
Very Expensive	over 800 francs
Expensive	400–800 francs
Moderate	200–400 francs
Inexpensive	under 200 francs

All prices are for a standard double room for two, including tax (18.6%) and service charge.

Bagnoles-de-l'Orne
Dining and Lodging
★

Le Manoir de Lys. Elegant guest rooms are decorated with flair at this magnificent Norman manor house, which lords it over a beautifully landscaped park on the edge of a forest. The restaurant has gained a considerable reputation for its cuisine *à la normande. Croix Gauthier, rte. de Juvigny (a mile from the casino), 61140, tel. 33–37–80–69. 20 rooms with bath. Facilities: restaurant, tennis. AE, MC, V. Closed Jan.–Feb.; restaurant closed Sun. dinner and Mon. Moderate–Expensive.*

Bois Joli. A less-imposing Norman manor house, Bois Joli has recently been renovated, and its cozily stylish guest rooms will make you feel right at home; they're all individually decorated. Peace and quiet reign here, and the delightful terrace overlooks the hotel's gardens. A piano plays softly in the background while diners tuck into good regional fare in the elegant restaurant. *12 av. Philippe-du-Rozier (opposite the race course), 61140, tel. 33–37–92–77. 20 rooms, 15 with bath. Facilities: restaurant, terrace, garden. AE, DC, MC, V. Restaurant closed mid-Nov.–mid-Mar. Moderate.*

Bayeux
Dining and Lodging

Le Lion d'Or. The Lion d'Or is a handsome '30s creation, conveniently situated in the center of town. Palm trees arch over the garden courtyard, while flowers cascade from balcony window boxes. The rooms are comfortable and well furnished with pretty fabrics. Fine Norman cuisine is served in the chic wood-beamed restaurant, decorated in shades of apricot. Specialties include *andouille chaude Bovary*, no doubt Madame Bovary's own recipe for hot sausages, and fillet of sole in a creamy lobster sauce. *71 rue St-Jean, 14400, tel. 31–92–06–90. 22 rooms with bath. Facilities: restaurant. AE, DC, MC, V. Closed Christmas–mid-Jan. Moderate.*

Lodging

Churchill. This small, stylish, friendly hotel opened in the town center in 1986 and has already made a mark with foreign visitors. Solid breakfasts (ham and eggs available on request) are served in the airy veranda. *14 rue St-Jean, 14400, tel. 31–21–31–80. 32 rooms with bath or shower. AE, DC, MC, V. Closed mid-Nov.–Mar. Moderate.*

★ **Hôtel d'Argouges.** This lovely 18th-century hotel is an oasis of calm in the city center, and many rooms offer views of the well-tended flower garden. The rooms are superb, tastefully furnished in French provincial chic and featuring rustic beamed ceilings. There's no restaurant. *21 rue St-Patrice, 14400, tel. 31–92–88–86. 22 rooms with bath. Facilities: garden. AE, DC, MC, V. Moderate.*

Le Bec-Hellouin
Dining and Lodging
★

Auberge de l'Abbaye. You'll enjoy traditional Norman cooking in this rustic inn, which features beamed ceilings and stone walls hung with ornamental copper pans. Charming Madame Sergent has been in charge for over a quarter of a century; she also has eight delightfully old-fashioned bedrooms but says they are reserved for her diners (though you don't have to stay here to eat at the restaurant). According to one famous TV personality, this restaurant serves the best apple tart in France. *Pl. de l'Eglise, 27800, tel. 32–44–86–02. Reservations advised. Dress: casual. MC, V. Closed Mon. and Tues. out of season and mid-Jan.–Feb. Moderate.*

Bénouville
Dining
★

Le Manoir d'Hastings. One of Normandy's most celebrated restaurants is situated in a little village 10 kilometers (6 miles) north of Caen. The 17th-century building was originally a Norman priory. In addition to the main dining room, there are 11 private rooms for more intimate (and expensive) occasions. Aperitifs and coffee are served in the garden. The considerable reputation of owner-chef José Aparicio is based mainly on his fish and seafood dishes. *18 av. de la Côte-de-Nacre, tel. 31–44–62–43. Reservations required. Jacket and tie required. AE, DC, MC, V. Closed Sun. dinner, Mon., and first half of Feb. Expensive.*

Bonsecours
Dining
★

Auberge de la Butte. Master chef Pierre Hervé is renowned for his subtle way with fish and seafood; his best dishes include poached oysters wrapped in spinach leaves and fricasseed fillet of sole. The magnificent Norman dining room's half-timbered walls are adorned with paintings and shining copper pots and pans, and the ceiling features exposed beams as well. *69 rte. de Paris, tel. 35–80–43–11. Reservations advised. Jacket and tie required. AE, DC, MC, V. Closed Sun., Mon., Dec. 22–Jan. 5, and Aug. Expensive.*

Cabourg
Lodging

Pullman Grand Hôtel. This luxurious, white-stucco hotel is set right on the seafront at the heart of town, and many guest rooms have balconies overlooking the sea. There's a lively piano bar during the summer season, and the hotel is connected to the casino. Its restaurant, Le Balbec, offers traditional French cuisine of a high standard but no great sophistication. *Promenade Marcel-Proust, 14390, tel. 31–91–01–79. 70 rooms with bath. Facilities: restaurant, bar. AE, DC, MC, V. Very Expensive.*

Caen
Dining
★

La Bourride. Normandy boasts a number of excellent restaurants; La Bourride, situated close to the castle down one of Caen's oldest streets, is one of the best. Chef Michel Bruneau's inventive and delicate dishes are inspired mainly by local produce, but the cooking is essentially modern. The small dining room is typically Norman, with stone walls, beamed ceilings, and a large fireplace. *15 rue du Vaugueux, tel. 31–93–50–76. Reservations required. Jacket and tie required. AE, DC, MC, V. Closed Sun., Mon., first 3 weeks in Jan. and second half of Aug. Expensive.*

Dining and Lodging
★

Château d'Audrieu. Nineteen kilometers (12 miles) west of Caen, on the road to Tilly-sur-Seulles, is a property that fulfills Hollywood's idea of a palatial château. A tree-lined avenue leads to an imposing, elegant 18th-century facade, which sets the tone for what lies within. The bedrooms and salons are the last word in Old World opulence, featuring wall sconces, overstuffed chairs, and antiques. The restaurant has an extensive wine list, and chef Alain Cornet uses produce from the château's own vegetable garden to create classic French dishes. *14250 Audrieu, tel. 31–80–21–52. 22 rooms with bath. Facilities: restaurant, bar, pool, park. MC, V. Closed Dec. 20–end Feb.; restaurant closed Wed., and Thurs. lunch. Expensive.*

★ **Le Dauphin.** Despite its downtown location—beware one-way streets as you arrive—Le Dauphin offers peace and quiet. The building is a former priory dating from the 12th century, though the smallish guest rooms are briskly modern. Those overlooking the street are soundproofed, while the rooms in back have views of the serene garden courtyard. The wood-beam breakfast room is a delightful place to start the day. The service is especially friendly and efficient, both in the hotel and in the excellent, though rather expensive, restaurant, which specializes in traditional Norman cooking. Fish is featured on the menu, though the veal sweetbreads in a mushroom sauce is a good choice as well. *29 rue Gémare, 14000, tel. 31–86–22–26. 22 rooms with bath or shower. Facilities: restaurant, garden. AE, DC, MC, V. Restaurant closed Sat. Moderate.*

Le Relais des Gourmets. One of the best hotels in town also has a terrific restaurant. The luxurious modern guest rooms are spacious and airy, and an Old World atmosphere reigns in the public rooms, which are dotted with charming antiques. The plush restaurant offers a sophisticated level of service and classic local cuisine. The gratinéed lobster with crayfish and turbot with cèpe mushrooms are memorable. Meals are served in the garden during summer months. *15 rue de Geôle, 14000, tel. 31–86–06–01. 32 rooms with bath. Facilities: restaurant, garden. AE, DC, MC, V. Restaurant closed Sun. dinner. Moderate.*

Deauville
Dining and Lodging

Normandy. The Normandy's exterior is a jet-set resort's idea of quaint: Gables and nooks create a sleek rendition of provincial style. Inside, the large guest rooms are rife with antiques and period-style furniture, and many overlook the sea. The restaurant extends into a Norman courtyard surrounded by apple trees. *38 rue Jean-Mermoz, 14800, tel. 31–98–66–22. 348 rooms, 290 with bath. Facilities: restaurant, garden. AE, DC, MC, V. Very Expensive.*

Le Royal. This gigantic five-star hotel, overlooking the sea and close to the casino, is stately and more than a trifle self-important. It has a range of guest rooms in various degrees of luxury and two restaurants: Le Royal, a sumptuous dining room in keeping with the establishment's general character, and L'Etrier, more intimate but still very plush, where the emphasis is on haute cuisine. *Blvd. Cornuché, 14800, tel. 31–98–66–33. 310 rooms, 281 with bath. Facilities: restaurants, pool, sauna, tennis. AE, DC, MC, V. Closed mid-Nov.–Easter. Very Expensive.*

Lodging

Le Continental. One of Deauville's oldest buildings is home to this provincial seaside hotel. The owner, Madame Perrot, is brisk and efficient, as is the service. The guest rooms are small and somewhat spartan—but this is Deauville, after all, and for the price you can't do much better. The Continental is handily placed between the port and the casino, but it doesn't have a restaurant. *1 rue Désiré-le-Hoc, 14800, tel. 31–88–21–06. 55 rooms, 36 with bath. AE, DC, MC, V. Closed mid-Nov.–mid-Mar. Inexpensive.*

Dieppe
Dining and Lodging

La Présidence. The modern Présidence overlooks the sea and offers airy, well-appointed guest rooms and an "English" bar, Le Verrazane. The delightful restaurant, Le Panoramic, is on the fourth floor, where classic, unpretentious, but tasty cooking predominates. *1 blvd. de Verdun, 76200, tel. 35–84–31–31. 88 rooms, 79 with bath. Facilities: restaurant. AE, DC, MC, V. Moderate.*

Duclair **Le Parc.** Pierre Le Patezour, one of the region's most acclaimed
Dining chefs, has created an excellent restaurant in Duclair, about 20 kilometers (12 miles) west of Rouen, on the road to Caudebec-en-Caux. The dining room features plush, Art Nouveau decor, and the menu offers such classic regional dishes as *canard à la Rouennaise* (duck in blood sauce). Le Patezour's subtle preparation of fillet of sole is an eye-opener. *721 av. du Président-Coty, tel. 35–37–50–31. Reservations advised. Jacket and tie required. AE, DC, MC, V. Closed Sun. dinner, Mon., and Dec. 20–Jan. 20. Expensive.*

Etretat **Les Roches Blanches.** Expect a warm welcome at this cozily un-
Dining pretentious family-run restaurant near the sea, which has three good-value menus. The house specialty is veal escalope with mushrooms, flambéed in Calvados, and there is a good range of fish and seafood dishes. *Rue Abbé-Cochet, tel. 35–27–07–34. Reservations advised, especially for Sun. lunch. Dress: casual. MC, V. Closed Tues., Wed., and Thurs. (Wed. only July–early Sept.), and Jan. and Oct. Moderate.*

Lodging **Le Donjon.** This charming little château is set in a large park overlooking the resort and offers lovely bay views. The individually furnished guest rooms are huge, comfortable, and quiet. Reliable French cuisine is served with flair in the cozy restaurant. *Chemin de St-Clair, 76790, tel. 35–27–08–23. 8 rooms, 6 with bath. Facilities: restaurant, pool. AE, DC, MC, V. Expensive.*

★ **Dormy House.** Thanks to its location halfway up the southern cliff, Dormy House provides dramatic views of the bay. Four buildings, dating from different periods and featuring a variety of architectural styles, make up the hotel. The large rooms are furnished in oak and sport cheerful floral drapes. Most guests stay on half-board; the restaurant specializes in fish and seafood. *Rte. du Havre, 76790, tel. 35–27–07–88. 32 rooms, 28 with bath. Facilities: restaurant. MC, V. Closed Jan.–mid-Mar. Moderate.*

Fécamp **Auberge de la Rouge.** The quaint Auberge de la Rouge is in a
Dining little hamlet a mile or so south of Fécamp. Its menu features a good mix of classic and modern dishes and includes many local specialties; the lobster is always a good bet. There are eight guest rooms, too. *Commune de St-Léonard, tel. 35–28–07–59. Reservations advised. Dress: casual. AE, DC, MC, V. Closed Sun. dinner and Mon. Moderate.*

★ **L'Escalier.** This delightfully simple little restaurant overlooks the harbor and serves traditional *cuisine à la normande.* The several inexpensive fixed-price menus mainly offer fish and seafood. *101 quai Bérigny, tel. 35–28–26–79. Reservations essential in summer. Dress: casual. DC, MC, V. Closed Mon. and 2 weeks in Nov. Inexpensive.*

Honfleur **L'Absinthe.** The Absinthe's 17th-century dining room, with
Dining stone walls and beamed ceilings, is a magnificent setting in which to enjoy chef Antoine Ceffrey's masterly creations, though on sunny days you'll probably want to eat outside on the terrace. Ceffrey has a delicate way with fish and seafood; try the *burbet,* a freshwater cod, prepared with ginger. *10 quai de*

la Quarantaine, tel. *31–89–39–00. Reservations advised. Jacket and tie required. AE, DC, MC, V. Closed Mon. evenings, Tues., and mid-Nov.–Christmas. Expensive.*

L'Ancrage. Massive seafood platters top the bill at this delightful old restaurant, which occupies a two-story 17th-century building overlooking the harbor. The cuisine is authentically Norman—simple but good. If you want a change from fish and seafood, try the succulent calf sweetbreads. *12 rue Montpensier, tel. 31–89–00–70. Reservations advised, especially in summer. Dress: casual. MC, V. Closed Tues. dinner, Wed., and Jan. Moderate.*

Dining and Lodging
★

Ferme St-Siméon. A 19th-century manor house—commonly held to be the birthplace of Impressionism—is set in the park that inspired such 19th-century luminaries as Claude Monet and Alfred Sisley. The guest rooms are individually decorated in a style an ad-man might term "palatial provincial," and a few have Jacuzzis. Pastel colors and floral wallpaper create a gardenlike aura in some rooms, while antiques and period decor are featured in others. The sophisticated restaurant specializes in fish, and in good weather you can eat out on the terrace. Save room for the extensive cheese board. *Rue Adolphe-Marais, on D513 to Trouville, 14600 Honfleur, tel. 31–89–23–61. 38 rooms with bath. Facilities: restaurant, tennis, park. MC, V. Restaurant closed Wed. lunch Nov.–Mar. Very Expensive.*

Auberge du Vieux Puits. Twenty kilometers (13 miles) southeast of Honfleur lies a quaint little cottage of a hotel, whose trellised and beamed exterior can't have changed much in the past 300 years. Early admirers included Gustave Flaubert, who gave the hotel a few lines in *Madame Bovary*. The guest rooms make use of heavy wooden furniture and pretty curtains and bedspreads to reflect the traditional feel of the architecture. The restaurant offers first-rate cuisine. *6 rue Notre-Dame-du-Pré, 27500 Pont-Audemer, tel. 32–41–01–48. 12 rooms, 6 with bath. MC, V. Closed Dec. 20–Jan. 22; restaurant closed Mon. evening and Tues. Moderate–Expensive.*

Le Cheval Blanc. Occupying a renovated, 15th-century building on the harborfront, this hotel has one of the finest restaurants in town. All the guest rooms have recently been redecorated and offer views of the port across the main road through town. Chef Christophe Bouvachon prepares classic yet delicate cuisine that is served with panache in the beautiful Louis XIII–style dining room. Try the seafood and oyster mousse or the sliced turbot in a subtle cider-and-cream sauce. *2 quai des Passagers, 14600, tel. 31–89–13–49. 35 rooms, 14 with bath. Facilities: restaurant. MC, V. Closed Jan.; restaurant (tel. 31–89–39–87) closed Wed. evening and Thurs. Moderate.*

Hostellerie Lechat. One of the best-known and loved establishments in Honfleur stands in a pretty square just behind the harbor in a typical 18th-century Norman building. The spacious guest rooms have recently been renovated in pretty French Provincial decor that makes good use of cheerful prints and colors. Foreign guests are given a warm welcome, especially in the American bar. The rustic, beamed restaurant serves top-notch Norman cuisine; lobster features prominently on the menu. *3 pl. Ste-Catherine, 14600, tel. 31–89–23–85. 24 rooms with bath. Facilities: restaurant, bar. AE, DC, MC, V. Restaurant closed Jan., Wed., and Thurs. lunch mid-Sept.–May. Moderate.*

Houlgate
Dining and Lodging

Mon Castel. If you want to stay on the Calvados coast but don't fancy pricey Deauville or Cabourg, cheerful Houlgate is your best bet. The down-to-earth Mon Castel offers the best value in town, especially if you secure the large-windowed room 1 on the second floor. Seafood reigns in the old-fashioned dining room. *1 blvd. des Belges, 14510, tel. 31–24–83–47. 12 rooms, some with bath or shower. MC, V. Inexpensive.*

Mont-St-Michel
Dining and Lodging
★

Mère Poulard. The hotel of the most celebrated restaurant on the mount consists of adjoining houses whose cozy, newly modernized, second-floor rooms are both comfortable and quiet. The restaurant's reputation derives partly from Mère Poulard's famous omelet (a recipe that originated in the 19th century and requires slow cooking over an open wood fire) and partly from its dramatic location. Young chef Jean-Luc Wahl successfully combines traditional and nouvelle cuisine, adding his own inventions to the long-standing house specialties. *50116 Mont-St-Michel, tel. 33–60–14–01. 26 rooms with bath. Facilities: piano bar, restaurant (reservations required). AE, DC, MC, V. Expensive.*

Terrasses Poulard. Monsieur Vannier bought this popular restaurant first and later acquired its more prestigious sister establishment (above). The hotel is a recent addition, a result of buying up and renovating the neighboring houses to create an ensemble of buildings that exude great charm and character, clustered around a small garden in the middle of the mount. The large restaurant attracts hordes of tourists; if you don't mind being surrounded by fellow Americans, Canadians, and Britons, you'll no doubt enjoy the traditional cuisine. *On the main road opposite the parish church, 50116, tel. 33–60–14–09. 29 rooms with bath. Facilities: restaurant, library, billiards room. AE, DC, MC, V. Moderate–Expensive.*

Rouen
Dining

La Couronne. The dining room of this 15th-century Norman building features beamed ceilings, leather-upholstered chairs, wood-paneled walls, and a scattering of sculpture. The traditional Norman cuisine makes few concessions to modernism; specialties include crayfish salad with foie gras and caviar, duck with orange, and turbot in puff pastry. *31 pl. du Vieux-Marché, tel. 35–71–40–90. Reservations advised. Jacket and tie required. AE, DC, MC, V. Expensive.*

La Grande Brasserie. A friendly, bustling bistro, La Grande Brasserie is located just beside the market and Joan of Arc's memorial church. It has a motherly staff and a huge menu with some worthwhile specialties. This is the place for succulent oysters and mussels and delicious tripe cooked the local way. There are tables outside in summer. *2 pl. du Vieux-Marché, tel. 35–15–14–24. Reservations advised. Dress: casual. AE, DC, V. Moderate.*

Dining and Lodging

Pullman Albane. This grandiose, modern (1976) hotel, just opposite the train station, has luxurious, comfortable rooms; the best feature '30s-style decor. There's an American bar, and the restaurant, Le Tournebroche, serves classic Norman cooking with creamy and cheesy sauces, as well as plain grilled and spit-roast dishes. *Rue Croix-de-Fer, 76000, tel. 35–52–69–52. 125 rooms with bath. Facilities: restaurant, bar. AE, DC, MC, V. Expensive.*

Hôtel de Dieppe. Dating from the late 19th century, the Dieppe remains fresh and up-to-date thanks to frequent redecoration. You can take your choice of rooms furnished in breezy modern

style or those with antique furniture. The restaurant, Les Qua-
tre Saisons, has a well-earned reputation and offers English-
style roasts, as well as such traditional French dishes as duck
cooked in its blood (which tastes much nicer than it sounds). *Pl.
Bernard-Tissot, 76000, tel. 35–71–96–00. 42 rooms with bath.
Facilities: restaurant, breakfast room. AE, DC, MC, V. Moderate.*

St-Valéry-en-Caux **Les Hêtres.** The most fashionable chef in Rouen has moved up
Dining the coast to Ingouville, just south of St-Valéry. Bertrand Warin
has created an elegant dining room that contrasts half-timbered walls and Louis XIII chairs with sleek modern furnishings. The tables are widely spaced, and large windows look out
onto an extensive landscaped garden. *Ingouville, tel. 35–57–
09–30. Reservations required. Jacket and tie required. No
credit cards. Closed Sun. evening, Mon., first half of Jan., and
last 2 weeks in Aug. Expensive.*

Trouville **Carmen.** This straightforward, unpretentious little hotel is
Lodging just around the corner from the casino. The rooms range from
the plain and inexpensive to the comfortable and moderate.
The restaurant offers good home cooking at value-for-the-mon-
ey prices. *24 rue Carnot, tel. 31–88–35–43. 14 rooms, 12 with
bath. Facilities: restaurant. AE, DC, MC, V. Closed Jan., part
of Apr., and third week in Oct. Restaurant closed Mon. dinner
and Tues. Inexpensive–Moderate.*

Vernon **Normandy.** Good accommodations near Giverny has long been
Dining and Lodging in short supply, so this hotel, opened in 1990, is good news. The
service is friendly, the breakfasts substantial, and the rooms
well equipped and calm (ask for one away from the street). *1 av.
Mendès-France, 27200, tel. 32–51–97–97. 50 rooms with bath.
Facilities: restaurant, bar. AE, MC, V. Moderate–Expensive.*

The Arts and Nightlife

The Arts

Music Normandy's cultural activities revolve around music, both classical and modern. Many churches host evening concerts, with
organ recitals drawing an especially large number of enthusiasts. Particularly good programs are featured at the church of
St-Ouen in Rouen, **St-Etienne** in Caen, and **St-Pierre** in Lisieux
(get details from the tourist office). Rouen's **St-Maclou** hosts an
annual series of organ recitals in August; even the venerable
abbey of **Mont-St-Michel** gets into the act during July and August. Jazz aficionados will be interested in the **European Traditional Jazz Festival** held in mid-June at Luneray, 8 kilometers (5
miles) southwest of Dieppe. For those who like spectacle with
their music, the **Théâtre des Arts** (tel. 35–71–41–36) in Rouen
stages numerous operas.

Festivals A **Joan of Arc Commemoration** takes place in Rouen at the end
of May, featuring a variety of parades, street plays, concerts,
and exhibitions that recall the life—and death—of France's patron saint.

Film One of the biggest cultural events on the Norman calendar is
the **American Film Festival**, held in Deauville during the first
week of September.

Nightlife

The hot spots of Normandy nightlife are, predictably enough, such resorts as Deauville, Trouville, and Cabourg, where discos and clubs vie with casinos for space.

Casinos The region is dotted with nearly 30 casinos, five of which—**Deauville, Forges-les-Eaux, Trouville, Dieppe,** and **Bagnoles-de-l'Orne**—rank among France's best, with floorshows and cabarets, as well as gaming rooms.

Bars and Nightclubs Try **Le Revoir** (14 bis rue Désiré-le-Hoc) in Deauville or Dieppe's **Casino** (3 blvd. de Verdun). Night owls will enjoy the smoky ambience of **Club Melody** in Deauville (13 rue Albert-Fracasse) and the jiving crowd at the **Green Onions Café** (29 blvd. des Belges) in Rouen.

4   Brittany

Rennes, Roscoff, Nantes

Thanks to its proximity to Great Britain, its folklore, and its spectacular coastline, Brittany (Bretagne in French) is a favorite destination among English-speaking vacationers. The French love the area, too, but don't worry about hordes of tourists—Brittany's vast beaches aren't easily crowded.

Occupying the bulbous portion of western France that juts far out into the Atlantic, the stubborn, independent-minded Bretons have more in common—both historically and linguistically—with the Celts of Cornwall, Wales, and Ireland than with their French countrymen. Both Brittany and Cornwall claim Merlin, King Arthur, and the Druids as cult figures, while huge Stonehenge-like menhirs and dolmens (prehistoric standing stones) litter the Breton countryside. As in Wales, nationalistic fervor has been channeled into gaining official acceptance for the local language.

Brittany became part of France in 1532, but regional folklore is still very much alive. An annual village *pardon* (a religious festival) will give you a good idea of Breton traditions: Banners and saintly statues are borne in colorful parades, accompanied by hymns, and the whole event is rounded off by food of all kinds. The most famous pardon is held on the last Sunday of August at Ste-Anne-la-Palud, near Quimper. The surrounding Finistère (from *Finis Terrae*, or Land's End) département, Brittany's westernmost district, is renowned for the costumes worn on such occasions—notably the lace bonnets, or *coiffes*, which can tower 15 inches above the wearer's head.

Geographically, Brittany is divided in two: maritime Armor ("land of the sea") and hinterland Argoat ("land of the forest"). The north of Brittany tends to be wilder than the south, where the countryside becomes softer as it descends toward Nantes and the Loire. Wherever you go, the coast is close by; the frenzied, cliff-bashing Atlantic surf alternates with sprawling beaches and bustling harbors. Islands, many inhabited and within easy reach of the mainland, dot the coastal waters.

Although Brittany's towns took a mighty hammering from the retreating Nazis in 1944, most have been tastefully restored, the large concrete-cluttered naval base at Brest being an exception. Rennes, the only Breton city with more than 200,000 inhabitants, retains its traditional charm, as do the towns of Dinan, Quimper, and Vannes. Many ancient man-made delights are found in the region's villages, often in the form of *calvaries* (ornate burial chapels). Other architectural highlights include castles and cathedrals, the most outstanding examples being those of Fougères and Dol, respectively.

Essential Information

Important Addresses and Numbers

Tourist Information The principal regional tourist offices are at **Rennes** (Pont de Nemours, tel. 99–79–01–98), **Brest** (8 av. Georges-Clemenceau, tel. 98–44–24–96), and **Nantes** (pl. du Commerce, tel. 40–47–04–51).

The addresses of other tourist offices in towns mentioned on this tour are as follows: **Carnac** (74 av. des Druides, tel. 97–52–13–52), **Concarneau** (quai d'Aiguillon, tel. 98–97–01–44),

Dinan (6 rue de l'Horloge, tel. 96–39–75–40), **Dinard** (2 blvd Féart, tel. 99–46–94–12), **Dol-de-Bretagne** (3 Grand Rue, tel. 99–48–15–37), **La Baule** (9 pl. de la Victoire, tel. 40–24–34–44), **Morlaix** (pl. des Otages, tel. 98–62–14–94), **Quiberon** (7 rue de Verdun, tel. 97–50–07–84), **Quimper** (rue de l'Amiral-de-la-Grandière, tel. 98–53–04–05), **St-Malo** (Esplanade St-Vincent, tel. 99–56–64–48), **Vannes** (1 rue Thiers, tel. 97–47–24–34), and **Vitré** (pl. St-Yves, tel. 99–75–04–46).

Travel Agencies **Wagons-Lits** (22 rue du Calvaire, Nantes, tel. 40–08–29–18 and 2 rue Jules-Simon, Rennes, tel. 99–79–45–96).

Car Rental **Avis** (pl. de la Gare, La Baule, tel. 40–60–36–28; 3 blvd. des Français-Libres, Brest, tel. 98–43–37–73; aéroport, Dinard, tel. 99–46–25–20; 18 blvd. de Stalingrad, Nantes, tel. 40–74–07–65; and 8 av. de la Gare, Quimper, tel. 98–90–31–34).

Arriving and Departing

By Plane There are domestic airports at Rennes, Brest, Nantes, Morlaix, Dinard, Quimper, and Lorient.

By Car Rennes, the gateway to Brittany, lies 368 kilometers (230 miles) west of Paris. It can be reached in about 4 hours, via Le Mans and the A81/A11 expressways (A11 continues from Le Mans to Nantes).

By Train There are numerous services daily between Paris (Gare Montparnasse) and Rennes (2 hours). Nantes is on a direct TGV line from Paris (250 miles in 2 hours).

Getting Around

By Car Rennes, a strategic base for penetrating Brittany, is linked by good roads to Morlaix and Brest (E50), Quimper (N24/N165), Vannes (N24/N166), Fougères (N12), and Dinan and St-Malo (N137).

By Train Some trains from Paris stop at Vitré before forking at Rennes on their way to either Brest (via Morlaix) or Quimper (via Vannes). Change at Rennes for Dol and St-Malo; at Dol for Dinan and Dinard (bus link); at Morlaix for Roscoff; at Rosporden, 19 kilometers (12 miles) south of Quimper, for Concarneau; and at Auray for Quiberon. There is regular train service down the west coast from Nantes to La Rochelle and Bordeaux.

Guided Tours

France Tourisme (3 rue de'Alger, 75001 Paris, tel. 42–61–85–50) organizes three-day tours of Normandy and Brittany from April through October. Sites include the châteaus on the Loire, Mont-St-Michel, and the walled city and spa town of St-Malo. The cost is 2,750 francs per person, with a single-room supplement of 370 francs. Further details of organized tours of Brittany can be had from the **Maison de la Bretagne** in Paris (Centre Commercial Maine-Montparnasse, 17 rue de l'Arrivée, B.P. 1006, 75737 Paris cedex 15, tel. 45–38–73–15) or from the regional tourist offices in Brest (tel. 98–44–24–96) and Quimper (tel. 98–53–04–05).

Exploring Brittany

Numbers in the margin correspond to points of interest on the Brittany map.

Orientation

Our first tour is confined to northeastern Brittany, which stretches from Rennes to the fortified harbor of St-Malo. This region played a frontline role in Brittany's efforts to repel French invaders during the Middle Ages, as can be seen in the massive castles of Vitré, Fougères, and Dinan. Our second tour begins 144 kilometers (90 miles) farther west, at the Channel port of Roscoff, before swinging southeast down the Atlantic coast to the city of Nantes at the mouth of the River Loire. Though Nantes is officially part of the Pays de la Loire, it has historic ties with Brittany, embodied in the imposing Château des Ducs de Bretagne.

Highlights for First-time Visitors

Menhirs and dolmens at Carnac, Tour 2
Ville Close, Concarneau, Tour 2
Dinan (Old Town), Tour 1
Nantes, Tour 2
Rennes, Tour 1
Vitré (Old Town), Tour 1
St-Malo (ramparts), Tour 1

Tour 1: Northeast Brittany

❶ Built high above the Vilaine Valley, **Vitré** (pronounced "vee-tray") is one of the age-old gateways to Brittany: There's still a feel of the Middle Ages about its dark, narrow alleys and tightly packed houses. The town's leading attraction is its formidable **castle**, shaped in an imposing triangle with fat, round towers. An 11th-century creation, it was first rebuilt in the 14th and 15th centuries to protect Brittany from invasion and proved to be one of the province's most successful fortresses: During the Hundred Years' War (1337–1453) the English repeatedly failed to take it, even though they occupied the rest of the town.

Time, not foreigners, came closest to ravaging the castle, which was heavily, though tastefully, restored during the past century. The town hall, however, is an unfortunate 1913 addition to the castle courtyard. You can visit the wing to the left of the entrance, beginning with the Tour St-Laurent and continuing along the walls via Tour de l'Argenterie, with its macabre collection of stuffed frogs and reptiles preserved in glass jars, to Tour de l'Oratoire. *Admission: 8 frs. Open Apr.–June, Wed.–Mon. 10–noon and 2:30–5:30, closed Tues; July–Sept., daily 10–noon and 1:30–6; Oct.–Mar., Wed.–Fri. 10–noon and 2–5:30, Mon. 2–5:30, closed Tues. and weekends.*

Vitré's castle is a splendid sight, especially from a vantage point on rue de Fougères across the river valley below. The castle stands at the west end of town, facing the narrow, cobbled streets of the remarkably preserved old town. Rue Poterie, rue d'En-Bas, and rue Beaudrairie, originally the home of tanners

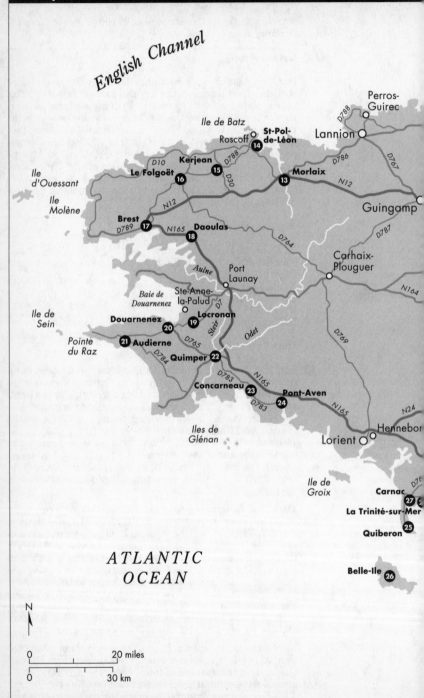

English Channel

Perros-
Guirec

Lannion

Ile de Batz

Roscoff
St-Pol-
de-Léon
14

*Ile
d'Ouessant*

Kerjean
15

Le Folgoët
16

D788

D30

Morlaix
13

N12

Guingamp

*Ile
Molène*

N12

Brest
17

D789

N165

Daoulas
18

D764

Carhaix-
Plouguer

D787

Aulne

Port
Launay

N164

*Baie de
Douarnenez*

Ste-Anne-
la-Palud

D7

Douarnenez
20

Locronan
19

*Ile de
Sein*

21 **Audierne**

D765

Steïr

Odet

D769

Pointe
du Raz

D784

Quimper
22

D783

N165

Concarneau
23

Pont-Aven
24

D783

N165

N24

*Iles de
Glénan*

Hennebor

Lorient

*Ile de
Groix*

Carnac

D7

27

La Trinité-sur-Mer

**ATLANTIC
OCEAN**

Quiberon

25

N
↑

Belle-Ile
26

0   20 miles

0   30 km

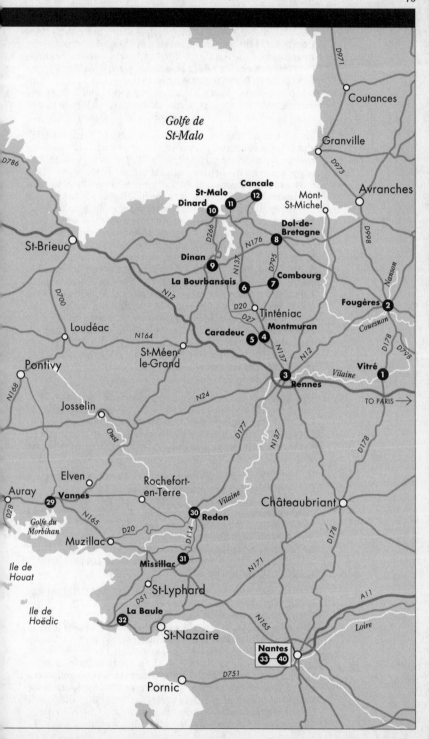

(the name comes from *baudoyers*—leather workers), make up a web of medieval streets as picturesque as any in Brittany; take time to stroll through them, soaking up the quaint atmosphere. Fragments of the town's medieval ramparts remain, including the 15th-century **Tour de la Bridolle** on place de la République, five blocks up from the castle. Built in the 15th and 16th centuries, **Notre-Dame** church has a fine, pinnacled south front and dominates a large square of the same name (you'll have passed it on the left on your way to place de la République).

Thirty-two kilometers (20 miles) due north of Vitré via D178 and D798 is **Fougères**, a traditional cobbling and cider-making center. For many centuries, it was a frontier town, valiantly attempting to guard Brittany against attack. Perhaps one of the reasons for its conspicuous lack of success is the site of the **castle:** Instead of sitting high up on the hill, it spreads out down in the valley, though the sinuous River Nançon does make an admirable moat. The 13-tower castle covers over five acres, making it one of the largest in Europe. Although largely in ruins, the castle is an excellent example of the military architecture of the Middle Ages, and it is impressive both inside and out. The thick walls—up to 20 feet across in places—were intended to resist 15th-century artillery fire, but the castle was to prove vulnerable to surprise attacks and sieges. A visit inside the castle walls reveals three lines of fortification, with the cosseted keep at their heart. There are charming views over Fougères from the Tour Mélusine and, in the Tour Raoul, a small shoe museum. The second and third stories of the Tour de Coigny were transformed into a chapel during the 16th century. *East end of town on pl. Raoul II. Admission: 12 frs. Open Apr.–Oct., daily 10–noon and 2–5; closed Nov.–Mar.*

The oldest streets of Fougères are alongside the castle, clustered around the elegant slate spire of **St-Sulpice** (rue de Lusignan), a Flamboyant Gothic church housing several fine altarpieces. A number of medieval houses line rue de la Pinterie, leading directly from the castle up to the undistinguished heart of town.

In the 1790s, Fougères was a center of Royalist resistance to the French Revolution. Much of the action in 19th-century novelist Honoré de Balzac's bloodcurdling novel *Les Chouans* takes place hereabouts; the novel's heroine, Marie de Verneuil, had rooms close to the church of **St-Léonard** (follow the river left from the castle), which overlooks the Nançon Valley. Both path and church, with its ornate facade and 17th-century tower, have changed little; the garden through which the path leads is known today as the **Jardin Public.**

Another man who was inspired by the scenery of Fougères was locally-born Emmanuel de La Villéon (1858–1944), a little-known Impressionist painter. His works are displayed in the **Musée La Villéon,** in one of the oldest surviving houses (dating from the 16th century) in hilltop Fougères; to reach it from the Jardin Public, head left past St-Léonard and cross the square into the adjacent rue Nationale. The more than 100 paintings, pastels, watercolors, and drawings suggest serene, underestimated talent. The artist's work ranges from compassionate studies of toiling peasants to pretty landscapes in which soft shades of green melt into hazy blue horizons. *51 rue Nationale. Admission: 8 frs. Open Easter–mid-June, weekends only, 11–*

12:30 and 2:30–5; mid-June–mid-Sept., weekdays 10:30–12:30 and 2:30–5:30, weekends and holidays 11–12:30 and 2:30–5.

❸ Rennes (pronounced "wren"), lying 48 kilometers (30 miles) southwest, is the traditional capital of Brittany. It has a different flavor from other towns in the region, mainly because of a terrible fire in 1720, which lasted a week and destroyed half the city. The remaining cobbled streets and half-timbered, 15th-century houses form an interesting contrast to the Classical feel of Jacques Gabriel's disciplined granite buildings, broad avenues, and spacious squares.

Start at the west end of the old town, bordered by the River Rance. The **Cathédrale St-Pierre,** a 19th-century building in Classical style that took 57 years to construct, looms above rue de la Monnaie. Stop in to admire its richly decorated interior and outstanding 16th-century Flemish altarpiece. *Pl. St-Pierre. Open Sept.–June, daily 8:30–noon and 2–5; July–Aug., Mon.–Sat. 8:30–noon and 2–5, Sun. 8:30–noon.*

Time Out The swinging youths of Rennes have a nighttime rendezvous at the **Babylone Bar** (12 rue des Dames), next to the cathedral. This isn't a place to linger in, but try it for a tangy, premeal aperitif or an end-of-evening, cream-and-brandy cocktail.

The surrounding streets are filled with 15th- and 16th-century houses in both medieval and Renaissance styles. Many have been converted into shops, boutiques, restaurants, and crepe houses; a lively **street market** is held in and around place des Lices on Saturday morning.

The pedestrian rue Lafayette and rue Nationale lead to the **Palais de Justice** (Law Courts). This palatial building, originally home to the Breton Parliament, was designed in 1618 by Salomon de Brosse, architect of the Luxembourg Palace in Paris, and was the most important building in Rennes to escape the 1720 fire. After admiring its white stone-and-granite facade, venture inside to view the splendid interior. Among its various magnificent halls is the richly carved and painted **Grand' Chambre,** a former parliamentary chamber whose walls are covered with Gobelin tapestries that retrace the history of Brittany. *Pl. du Parlement. Admission: 15 frs. Open Wed.–Mon. 10–noon and 2–6; closed Tues.*

Head down from the Palais de Justice and left across quai Émile-Zola to the **Palais des Musées,** a huge building containing two museums—the **Musée des Beaux-Arts** and **Musée de Bretagne.** The Fine Arts Museum on the second floor houses one of the country's best collections of paintings outside Paris, featuring works by Georges de la Tour, Jean-Baptiste Chardin, Camille Corot, Paul Gauguin, and Maurice Utrillo, to name only a few. The ground-floor Museum of Brittany retraces the region's history, period by period, by way of costumes, models, porcelain, furniture, coins, statues, and shiny push-button visual displays. *20 quai Émile-Zola. Admission: joint ticket 18 frs. adults, 9 frs. children under 14. Open Wed.–Mon. 10–noon and 2–6. Closed holidays.*

Northeast of the museum building, a five-minute walk via rue Gambetta and rue Victor-Hugo, is the **Jardin du Thabor,** a large, formal French garden with regimented rows of trees, shrubs, and flowers. Even the lawns are manicured—not often

the case in France. There is a notable view of the church of
Notre-Dame-en-St-Mélaine in one corner.

North of Rennes, the landscape is dotted with hefty castles and
enticing châteaus. Twenty-four kilometers (15 miles) away via
④ N137 and D27 is the castle of **Montmuran**, closely associated
with Brittany's warrior-hero Bertrand du Guesclin; here, he
was knighted in 1354 and married his second wife in 1372. An
alley of oak and beech trees leads up to the main 18th-century
building, which is surrounded by a moat and flanked by four
towers, two built in the 12th century, two in the 14th. You can
visit the towers and a small museum devoted to the castle's history. *Admission: 16 frs. Open Easter–Oct., daily 2–7; Nov.–
Easter, weekends only, 2–6.*

⑤ Just 8 kilometers (5 miles) west is **Caradeuc,** a Classical château
ambitiously dubbed the "Versailles of Brittany." Visitors can't
go inside to check out this claim, unfortunately, but to compensate, explore the surrounding park—Brittany's largest—and
admire its statues, flower beds, and leafy alleys. *Admission: 12
frs. Open Apr.–Oct., daily 9–noon and 1:30–8; Nov.–Mar.,
weekends only, 2–6.*

⑥ Take D20 to Tinténiac, then N137 north to **La Bourbansais**, a
total of 19 kilometers (12 miles) from Caradeuc. This castle has
remained in the same family since it was founded by local lord
Jean de Breil in 1583. It, too, has extensive gardens, containing
a small zoo and a pack of hunting hounds. The buildings were
enlarged in the 18th century, and the majority of the interior
furnishings date from that period. There are fine collections of
porcelain and tapestries. *Admission: 32 frs. Castle open Apr.–
Oct., daily 2–6; Nov.–Mar., weekends only, 2–6. Park open
daily 10–noon and 2–7.*

⑦ **Combourg**, best known as the boyhood home of Romantic writer viscount Chateaubriand (1768–1848), is 11 kilometers (7
miles) east along D75 and D794. The thick-walled, four-tower
castle dates mainly from the 14th and 15th centuries and contains a roomful of Chateaubriand archives. You can visit the
writer's austere bedroom in the Tour du Chat (Cat's Tower).
The castle grounds—ponds, woods, and half-tended lawns—
are suitably mournful and can seem positively desolate under
leaden skies. *Admission: 22 frs., park only 11 frs. Castle open
Mar.–Nov., Wed.–Mon. 2–5; closed Tues. Park open Mar.–
Nov., Wed.–Mon. 9–noon and 2–5.*

⑧ Seventeen kilometers (10 miles) north via D795, the ancient
town of **Dol-de-Bretagne** looks out from its 60-foot cliffs over Le
Marais, a marshy plain stretching across to Mont-St-Michel, 21
kilometers (13 miles) northeast. The **Promenade des Douves**,
laid out along the northern part of the original ramparts, offers
extensive views of Le Marais and Mont Dol, a 200-foot granite
mound, 3 kilometers (2 miles) north, legendary scene of combat
between St. Michael and the devil. Unfortunately, the stately
trees that line the promenade suffered heavy damages in a 1987
hurricane.

At the end of the promenade, note the **Cathédrale St-Samson**
(pl. de la Cathédrale), a damp, soaring, fortresslike bulk of
granite dating mainly from the 12th to the 14th centuries. This
mighty building shows just how influential the bishopric of Dol
was in days gone by. The richly sculpted Great Porch, carved

wooden choir stalls, and stained glass in the chancel deserve
close scrutiny.

Turn down rue des Écoles to the small **Musée Historique d'Art
Populaire.** During a short, cheerful guided tour, you'll see costumes, weapons, and a series of scale models retracing life in
Dol since prehistoric times. The glory of the museum, though,
is its assembly of colored wooden religious statues. *Rue des
Écoles. Admission: 14 frs. Open Apr.–Sept., Wed.–Mon. 10–5;
closed Tues.*

Rue des Écoles leads to Dol's picturesque main street, Grand-
Rue des Stuarts, lined with medieval houses. The oldest, at No.
17, boasts a chunky row of Romanesque arches.

⑨ From Dol, take N176 to **Dinan,** 24 kilometers (15 miles) southwest. Dinan has close links with Brittany's 14th-century anti-
English warrior-hero Bertrand du Guesclin, whose name is
commemorated in countless squares and hostelries across the
province. Du Guesclin won a famous victory here in 1359 and
promptly married a local girl, Tiphaine Raguenel. When he
died in the siege of Auvergne (central France) in 1380, his body
was dispatched home to Dinan. Owing to the great man's popu-
larity, however, only his heart completed the journey—the
rest of him having been confiscated by devoted followers in
towns along the route.

Begin your stroll around the old town at the tourist office,
housed in a charming 16th-century building in rue de l'Horloge.
For a superb view of the town, climb to the top of the nearby
belfry, the **Tour de l'Horloge.** *Admission: 5 frs. Open July–
Aug., Mon.–Sat. 10–noon and 2–6.*

Turn left and head half a block along to admire the triangular-
gabled wooden houses in **place des Merciers, rue de l'Apport,** and
rue de la Poissonnerie. With their overhanging balconies and
black-and-white half-timbered houses, these cobbled streets
are so pretty you may think you've stumbled into a Hollywood
movie set. Restore your faith with a visit to the nearby church,
the **Basilique St-Sauveur** (turn right out of place des Merciers
along rue Haute-Voie, then take the second left into the church
square). The church is a mixture of styles, ranging from the Romanesque south front to the Flamboyant Gothic facade and
Renaissance side chapels. Du Guesclin's heart lies in the north
transept.

The **Jardin Anglais** (English Garden) is just behind the church;
it's not really much of a garden, but its old trees nicely frame
the east end of St-Sauveur. More spectacular views can be
found at the bottom of the garden, which looks down the plum-
meting Rance Valley to the river 250 feet below.

Leading down to the harbor, rue du Jerzual is a beautifully preserved medieval street, filled with boutiques and crafts shops,
divided halfway down by the town walls and massive Porte du
Jerzual gateway.

Time Out Wool yarn by the yard and English cakes and scones by the doz-
en: That's the unlikely combination you'll find at this strange
little American-run outfit, **La Toison d'Or** (rue du Jerzual),
long wooden benches add to the atmosphere, if not the comfort,
as you settle down for a cup of coffee and a snack.

Dinan's harbor seems somewhat forlorn; although there are sailings in summer up the River Rance to Dinard and St-Malo, abandoned warehouses bear witness to vanished commercial activity, with only an occasional restaurant to brighten up the place.

Time Out Just across the Vieux Pont, in what is officially the village of Lanvallay, is **Le Transfert** cocktail bar, whose cool-gray decor wouldn't be out of place in some trendy *quartier* of Paris. The cocktails are imaginative and inexpensive, and you can enjoy them in peace and quiet while drinking in the tranquil views over the River Rance and the old part of Dinan. *8 bis rue du Four, Lanvallay. Open 6* PM–*2* AM.

Amble back up the hill (it's steep) and turn right, well after the Porte du Jerzual, into rue de l'École. This street leads down to another gateway, the Porte St-Malo, from which the leafy Promenade des Grands Fossés heads left on a tour of the best-preserved section of the town walls. Follow these walls around as far as the **castle.** Here you can visit the two-story Coëtquen Tower and 100-foot 14th-century keep, containing varied displays of medieval effigies and statues, Breton furniture, and local *coiffes* (bonnets). *Porte de Guichet. Admission: 14 frs. Open June–Aug., 9–noon and 2–7, Sept.–Oct. and Mar.–May, 9–noon and 2–6, Nov.–Feb., 2–5; closed Tues.*

⑩ Dinard is the most elegant resort on this stretch of the Brittany coast. It's only 22 kilometers (14 miles) north on D266, but a bit farther away if you follow the picturesque meanderings of the Rance. The town's picture-book setting on the Rance Estuary opposite the walled city of St-Malo is probably what lured the English aristocracy here in droves after it was discovered by an American named Coppinger. What started out as a small fishing port soon became a seaside mecca of lavish turn-of-the-century villas, grand hotels, and a bustling casino. A number of more modern establishments punctuate the landscape, but the town still retains something of an Edwardian tone. Walking along Dinard's sandy, crescent-shaped beaches, it's easy to see why upper-crust Edwardians loved the place.

To make the most of Dinard's exhilarating setting, head down to the town's southern tip, the **Pointe de la Vicomté,** where cliffs offer panoramic views across the Baie du Prieuré and Rance Estuary. The **Plage du Prieuré,** named after a priory that once stood here, is a sandy beach ringed by yachts, dinghies, and motorboats. The **Clair de Lune Promenade** hugs the seacoast on its way toward the English Channel, passing in front of the small jetty used by boats crossing to St-Malo. Shortly after, the street reaches the **Musée de la Mer** (Marine Museum and Aquarium). Virtually every known species of Breton bird and sea creature is on display here, in two rooms and 24 pools. Another room is devoted to the polar expeditions of explorer Jean Charcot, one of the first men to chart the Antarctic; there are poignant souvenirs of his last voyage, in 1936, from which he never returned. *Claire de Lune Promenade. Admission: 10 frs. Open Pentecost Sun.–Sept., daily 10–noon and 2–6.*

The Clair de Lune Promenade, lined with luxuriant semitropical vegetation, really hits its stride as it rounds the Pointe du Moulinet to the Prieuré Beach. River meets sea in a foaming mass of rock-pounding surf, and caution is needed as you walk along the slippery path. Your reward: the calm and shelter of the **Plage de l'Écluse,** an inviting sandy beach, bordered by a casino and numerous stylish hotels. The coastal path picks up again on the far side, ringing the Pointe de la Malouine and Pointe des Etêtés before arriving at Dinard's final beach, the **Plage de St-Enogat.**

⑪ Little more than a mile from Dinard by water, but 13 kilometers (8 miles) by road, is the ancient walled town of **St-Malo.** The stone ramparts of this onetime pirate base have stood firm against the Atlantic since the 13th century. The town itself has proved less resistant: A week-long fire in 1944, kindled by retreating Nazis, wiped out nearly all the old buildings. Restoration work was more painstaking than brilliant, but the narrow streets and granite houses of the old town, known as *Intra Muros* ("within the walls") have been satisfactorily re-created, enabling St-Malo to regain its role as a busy fishing port and seaside resort.

North American visitors can pay homage to Jacques Cartier, who set sail from St-Malo in 1535 to discover the St. Lawrence River and found Quebec. Cartier's tomb is in the church of **St-Vincent** (off Grande-Rue), while his statue looks out over the town ramparts, four blocks away—along with that of swashbuckling corsair Robert Surcouf, hero of many daring 18th-century raids on the British navy (he's the one pointing an accusing finger over the waves at *l'Angleterre*). The ramparts themselves date from the 12th century, but were considerably enlarged and modified in the 18th century. They extend from the castle in St-Malo's northeast corner and ring the old town, with a total length of over a mile. The views from the ramparts are stupendous, especially at high tide. Five hundred yards offshore is the **Ile du Grand Bé,** a small island housing the somber military tomb of viscount Chateaubriand, who was born in St-Malo. The islet can be reached by a causeway at low tide, as can the **Fort National,** a massive fortress with a dungeon constructed in 1689 by that military-engineering genius Sébastien de Vauban. *By the castle. Admission: 8 frs. Open Apr.–Sept., daily 9:30–noon and 2:30–6.*

At the edge of the ramparts, overlooking the Fort National, is **St-Malo Castle,** whose great keep and watchtowers command an impressive view of the harbor and coastline. The castle houses two museums: the **Musée de la Ville,** devoted to local history, and the **Quic-en-Grogne,** a tower where various episodes and celebrities from St-Malo's past are recalled by way of waxwork reconstruction. *Porte St-Vincent. Admission: 10 frs. (Musée de la Ville), 15 frs. (Quic-en-Grogne). Open May–Sept., daily 9:30–noon and 2–6:30; Apr. and Oct., daily 10–noon and 2–6; closed Tues. Nov.–Mar.*

⑫ Anyone who enjoys eating oysters should make the 13-kilometer (8-mile) trip east on D355 to **Cancale,** renowned for its oyster beds. You'll find lots of quayside restaurants in which to sample this delicacy. The town's delightful seaside setting is also an attraction.

Tour 2: Brittany's Western Coast

⑬ Our second tour begins at **Morlaix** (pronounced "Morley"), far to the west of St-Malo—144 kilometers (90 miles) by fast N12, considerably longer if you meander along the spectacular coastal road (D786 and D788) via Perros-Guirec and Lannion. Morlaix's town-spanning, 19th-century, two-tiered rail viaduct is an unforgettable sight—300 yards long and 200 feet high. Though there are no major sights in Morlaix, the old town is an attractive mix of half-timbered houses and low-fronted shops that rewards unhurried exploration. The pedestrian Grand' Rue is its commercial heart, lined with quaint 15th-century houses. The **Maison de la Reine Anne,** in adjacent rue du Mur, is a three-story 16th-century building adorned with statuettes of saints. It has been undergoing restoration, so access may be limited.

Just off rue d'Aiguillon, which runs parallel to Grand' Rue, is the town museum, known as the **Musée des Jacobins** because it is housed in the former Jacobin church; an early 15th-century rose window survives at one end as a reminder. The museum's eclectic display ranges from religious statues to archaeological findings and modern paintings. *Pl. des Jacobins. Admission: 10 frs. Open July–Aug., daily 10–noon and 2–6; Apr.–June and Sept.–Oct., Wed.–Mon. 10–noon and 2–6; Nov.–Mar., Wed.–Mon. 10–noon and 2–5.*

(14) D73 hugs the riverbank north of Morlaix; branch left at Kerdanet and follow signs for **St-Pol-de-Léon,** 10 kilometers (6 miles) farther away. St-Pol is a lively market town dominated by three spires: Two belong to the cathedral, the highest to the Chapelle du Kreisker. The **Ancienne Cathédrale,** built between the 13th and 16th centuries, is pleasingly proportioned, and its finely carved 16th-century choir stalls are worth a trip inside. Rue du Général-Leclerc, with its large wood-framed houses, links the cathedral to the **Chapelle du Kreisker,** originally used for meetings by the town council. Its magnificent 250-foot 15th-century granite spire, flanked at each corner by tiny spirelets known as *fillettes* ("young girls"), is the prototype for countless bell towers in Brittany. From the top there is a rewarding view across the Bay of Morlaix toward the English Channel. *Access to the tower mid-June–mid-Sept., daily 10–noon and 2–5. Admission: 5 frs.*

(15) Just 5 kilometers (3 miles) north of St-Pol along D58 is the burgeoning port of Roscoff. From here, head 24 kilometers (15 miles) southwest toward Brest before turning right onto D30 and making for the nearby 15th-century château of **Kerjean.** With its vast park, ditch, and 40-foot-thick defensive walls, Kerjean at first looks like a fortress until you see the large windows, tall chimney stacks, and high-pitched roofs of its main buildings. The chapel, kitchens, and main apartments, full of regional furniture, can be visited. Temporary exhibitions are held in the stable wing. Notice the old well in the main courtyard. *Admission: 22 frs. Open Sept.–June, Wed.–Mon. 10–noon and 2–7; July–Aug., Wed.–Mon. 10–7.*

(16) Sixteen kilometers (10 miles) west of Kerjean along D788 is **Le Folgoët** and its splendid **Notre-Dame basilica,** whose sturdy north tower, visible from afar, beckons pilgrims to the *pardon* (religious festival) held here in early September. On this occasion, many pilgrims drink at the Salaün fountain against the wall behind the church; its water comes from a spring beneath the altar, which can be reached through a sculpted porch. Inside the church is a rare, intricately worked, granite rood-screen separating the choir and nave.

⑰ Continue along D788 to the maritime city of **Brest**, 24 kilometers (15 miles) southwest. Brest's enormous, sheltered bay is strategically positioned close to the Atlantic and the English Channel. During World War II, Brest was used by the Germans as a naval base; it was liberated in 1944 by American forces, after a 43-day siege that left the city in ruins. Postwar reconstruction, resulting in long, straight streets of reinforced concrete, has left latter-day Brest with the unenviable reputation of being one of France's ugliest cities. Its waterfront, however, is worth visiting for the few old buildings and museums, as well as for dramatic views across the bay toward the Plougastel Peninsula.

Begin your visit at one of the town's oldest monuments, the **Tour Tanguy**. This bulky, round 14th-century tower, once used as a lookout post, is a majestic sight in its own right; the interior contains a museum of local history with scale models of the Brest of yore. *Admission free. Open Oct.–May, Thurs. and weekends 2–6; June and Sept., daily 2–7; July–Aug., daily 10–noon and 2–7.*

Next to the tower is the River Penfeld and, crossing it, the Pont de Recouvrance, at 95 yards Europe's longest lift-bridge. On the other side, Brest's medieval castle is home to the **Musée de la Marine** (Naval Museum), containing boat models, sculpture, pictures, and naval instruments. A section is devoted to the castle's 700-year history. The dungeons can also be visited. *Admission: 18 frs. adults, 9 frs. children under 12. Open Wed.–Mon. 9:15–noon and 2:20–6; closed Tues.*

A short walk inland leads to the **Musée Municipal** in rue Traverse. French, Flemish, and Italian paintings, spanning the period from the 17th to the 20th century, make up the collection. *Rue Émile-Zola. Admission free. Open Wed.–Sat. and Mon. 10–11:45 and 2–6:45, Sun. 2–6:45; closed Tues.*

Farther east, overlooking the Moulin Blanc marina, is the brand-new, futuristic **Océanopolis** center. Maritime technology, fauna, and flora are the themes of its exhibits, but the biggest attraction is the aquarium—the largest in Europe. *Rue Alain-Colas. Admission: 40 frs. Open Tues.–Sun. 10–12 and 2–6.*

⑱ Southbound N165, which leaves Brest for Quimper, 104 kilometers (65 miles) away, soon passes through **Daoulas,** where you can stop off to admire the *Enclos Paroissial* (literally, "parish enclosure") and the 12th-century Romanesque abbey, with its cloisters and herbal garden. Stay on N165 until you reach Port Launay, then branch off southwest along scenic D7 to ⑲ **Locronan**, a typical old weaving town with a magnificently preserved ensemble of houses, main square, and 15th-century church.

Before heading south on D7, you may want to head toward the coast for some fresh sea air and a look at Brittany as it has been for centuries. As you approach the cliffs and inlets of **Ste-Anne-la-Palud,** the roads become blissfully free of cars and are lined with the charming stone cottages that are typical of the area.

⑳ **Douarnenez**, 10 kilometers (6 miles) west of Locronan via D7, is a quaint old fishing town of quayside paths and narrow streets. Sailing enthusiasts will be interested in the town's biennial classic boat rally in mid-August (the next event takes place in

1994), when traditionally rigged sailing boats of every description ply the waters of the picturesque Bay of Douarnenez.

Due west of Douarnenez, parts of the coast look more like the breezy bluffs of Ireland than like France, especially around **Pointe du Raz.** This is the westernmost tip of the country, marked by a dramatic 300-foot drop; the spectacular view is worth the detour. Just south of Pointe du Raz is the small, ㉑ working port of **Audierne,** where the fishermen come daily bearing the day's catch of langoustines. In summer, it is a busy pleasure-boat center that is never overcrowded; most of the visitors are locals, which makes for a nontouristy, welcoming atmosphere.

㉒ From Douarnenez, take D765 southeast to **Quimper.** This lively commercial town is the ancient capital of the Cornouaille province, founded, it is said, by King Gradlon 1,500 years ago. Quimper (pronounced "cam-pair") owes its strange-looking name to its site at the confluence *(kemper* in Breton) of the Odet and Steir rivers. The banks of the Odet are a charming place for strolling. Highlights of the old town include **rue Kéréon,** a lively shopping street, and the stately **Jardin de l'Evêché** (Bishop's Gardens) behind the cathedral in the center of the old town.

The **Cathédrale St-Corentin** is a masterpiece of Gothic architecture and the second-largest cathedral in Brittany (after that of Dol). Legendary King Gradlon is represented on horseback just below the base of the spires, harmonious mid-19th-century dditions to the medieval ensemble. The luminous 15th-century stained glass is particularly striking. *Pl. St-Corentin.*

Two museums flank the cathedral. Works by major masters, such as Rubens, Corot, and Picasso, mingle with pretty landscapes from the local Gauguin-inspired Pont-Aven school in the **Musée des Beaux-Arts** (Fine Arts Museum; admission 20 frs.; open Wed.–Mon. 9:30–noon and 1–5), while local furniture, ceramics, and folklore top the bill in the **Musée Départemental** (Regional Museum) in adjacent rue du Roi-Gradlon *(admission 10 frs.; open mid-Sept.–Apr., Wed.–Sun. 9:30–noon and 2–6, May–mid-Sept., Wed.–Mon. 9:30–noon and 2–6:30).*

Quimper sprang to nationwide attention as an earthenware center in the mid-18th century, when it began producing second-rate imitations of the Rouen ceramics known as faïence, featuring blue Oriental motifs. Today's more colorful designs, based on floral arrangements and marine fauna, are still often handpainted. There are guided visits to the main pottery, the **Faïencerie Henriot,** and its museum, situated on the banks of the Odet south of the old town. *Allée de Locmaria. Admission: 12 frs. Open Mon.–Thurs. 9:30–11 and 1:30–4:30; Fri. 9:30–11 and 1:30–3.*

㉓ **Concarneau,** 21 kilometers (13 miles) from Quimper along D783, is the third-largest fishing port in France. A busy industrial town, it has a grain of charm and an abundance of tacky souvenir shops. The town's main attraction, the **Ville Close,** is a fortified islet in the middle of the harbor that you enter by a quaint drawbridge. The view of the harbor from here is splendid. From early medieval times, Concarneau was regarded as impregnable, and the fortifications were further strengthened by the English under John de Montfort during the War of Succession (1341–64). This enabled the English-controlled Concarneau to withstand two sieges by Breton hero Bertrand

du Guesclin; the third siege was successful for the plucky du
Guesclin, who drove out the English in 1373. Three hundred
years later, Sébastien de Vauban remodeled the ramparts into
what you see today: half a mile long and highly scenic, offering
views across the two harbors on either side of the Ville Close.
*Admission to ramparts: 5 frs. Open Easter–Sept., daily 9–7;
winter 10–5.*

At the end of rue Vauban closest to the drawbridge is the **Musée
de la Pêche** (Fishing Museum), which houses aquariums and offers historical explanations of fishing techniques around the
world. *Admission: 25 frs. Open Sept.–June, daily 10–12:30
and 2–7; July–Aug., daily 10–6.*

If you're in Concarneau during the second half of August, you
will be able to enjoy the Fête des Filets Bleus (Blue Net Festival) in the Ville Close. This festival is a week-long folk celebration in which Bretons in costume swirl and dance to the wail of
bagpipes.

24 **Pont-Aven,** just a few kilometers down coastal backroads or
D783, is a former artists' colony that was headquarters for Paul
Gauguin before he headed off to the exotica of the South Seas.
The group was known as the Pont-Aven School, and the **Musée
Municipal** has a permanent photography exhibition document-
ing it all, as well as shows of different artists who participated
in the movement. *Pl. de l'Hotel de Ville, tel. 98–06–14–43. Ad-
mission: 20 frs. July–Aug., 12 frs. Apr.–June and Sept.–Dec.
Open Apr.–Dec.*

Boat trips down the estuary from Pont-Aven are a relaxing way
to cool off in summer breezes, or you can walk up a hill among
the pastures to the Tremalo chapel, where there is a crucifix
that has been attributed to Gauguin.

N165 speeds down the coast, past the industrial port of Lorient, as far as Auray. Here, take D768 southwest toward Carnac at the northern end of the 10-mile-long Quiberon Peninsula,
dangling off the Brittany coast. The Côte Sauvage (Wild Coast)
on the west of the peninsula is a savage mix of crevices, coves,
and rocky grottoes lashed by violent seas.

25 **Quiberon** itself is famed for more soothing waters: It is a spa
town with fine, relaxing beaches.

Time Out   In a country where gourmandism is virtually a cultural pursuit,
Henri Le Roux (18 rue du Port-Maria) has taken the art of
chocolateering to dizzying heights. Check out his delicious displays—created before your very eyes—at his shop near Quiberon Harbor.

The cheerful harbor of Port-Maria is the base for boat trips to
nearby Belle-Ile, at 11 miles long the largest of Brittany's islands. Because of the cost and inconvenience of reserving car-
berths on the ferry, it's best to cross to Belle-Ile as a pedestrian
and rent a car—or, better still, a bicycle—on the island.

Despite being a mere 45-minute boat trip from Quiberon,
26 **Belle-Ile** is much less commercialized, and exhilarating scenery
is its main appeal. Near Sauzon, the island's prettiest settle-
ment, is a view across to the Quiberon Peninsula and Gulf of
Morbihan from the **Pointe des Poulains,** home of Belle Epoque
actress Sarah Bernhardt. The nearby **Grotte de l'Apothicairerie**

is a grotto whose name derives from the local cormorants' nests, said to resemble pharmacy bottles. Farther south, near Port Goulphar, is another dramatic sight—the **Grand Phare** (lighthouse), built in 1835 and rising 275 feet above sea level. Its light is one of the most powerful in Europe, visible from 75 miles across the Atlantic. If the keeper is available, you may be able to climb to the top and admire the view.

27 Once back on the mainland, return to **Carnac** at the north end of Quiberon Bay. Carnac is famed for its beaches and, especially, its **megalithic monuments** dating from the Neolithic/Early Bronze Ages (3500–1800 BC). The whys and wherefores of their construction remain as obscure as those of their English contemporary, Stonehenge, although religious beliefs and astrology were doubtless an influence. The 2,395 menhirs that make up the three *Alignements* (Kermario, Kerlescan, and Ménec) are positioned with astounding astronomical accuracy in semicircles and parallel lines over half a mile long. There are also smaller-scale dolmen ensembles and three tumuli (mounds or barrows), including the 130-yard-long **Tumulus de St-Michel**, topped by a small chapel affording fine views of the rock-strewn countryside. *Guided tours of the tumulus daily Apr.–Sept. Cost: 5 frs.*

28 Just east of Carnac lies the yachtsman's paradise of **La Trinité-sur-Mer**, a resort town ringed by sandy beaches and oyster beds, and much favored by wealthy Parisians seeking a home-away-from-home vacation. From La Trinité, head up D781 and **29** D28 to Auray, then take N165 east to **Vannes** (pronounced "van"). Scene of the declaration of unity between France and Brittany in 1532, Vannes is one of the few towns in Brittany to have been spared damage during World War II, so its authentic regional charm remains intact. Be sure to visit the **Cohue** (medieval market hall—now a temporary exhibition center) and the picturesque **place Henri IV** and browse in the small boutiques and antiques shops in the surrounding pedestrian streets. The ramparts, Promenade de la Garenne, and medieval washhouses are all set against the backdrop of the much-restored **Cathédrale St-Pierre**, with its 1537 Renaissance chapel, Flamboyant Gothic transept portal, and treasury in the old chapterhouse. *Pl. du Cathédrale. Admission: 3 frs. Treasury open mid-June–mid-Sept., Mon.–Sat. 10–noon and 2–6.*

From Vannes, N165 goes to Muzillac, 19 kilometers (12 miles) away, from which D20 veers 43 kilometers (27 miles) east to the **30** little town of **Redon,** built at the junction of the River Vilaine and the Nantes–Brest canal. These days, Redon Harbor is used exclusively by pleasure boats, but it was once a busy commercial port. A number of stylish 17th–19th-century mansions, with large windows and wrought-iron balconies, line the adjacent quays. Wood-framed medieval houses line the main street, Grande Rue, which is dominated by the slender spire and magnificent Romanesque tower of the church of **St-Sauveur,** all that remains of a once-powerful Benedictine abbey.

31 Head due south from Redon, via D114, to **Missillac,** at the edge of the **Grande Brière Regional Park.** This low-lying marshy area, crisscrossed by narrow canals, can be explored either by boat (trips are organized from St-Nazaire) or by car along D51 as you head southwest toward La Baule. Ever since a ducal edict of 1461, La Brière has been the common property of its inhabitants, who live in distinctive and picturesque white thatched cottages. Highlights include the panoramic view from the church tower at **St-Lyphard** and the curious **Kerbourg dolmen** 5 kilometers (3 miles) south, just off D47.

㉜ La Baule, 18 kilometers (11 miles) from St-Lyphard, is one of the most fashionable resorts in France. Like Le Touquet and Dinard, it is a 19th-century creation, founded in 1879 to make the most of the excellent sandy beaches that extend 6 miles around the broad, sheltered bay between Pornichet and Le Pouliguen. A pine forest, planted in 1840, keeps the shifting local sand dunes firmly at bay.

An air of old-fashioned chic still pervades La Baule's palatial hotels, villas, and flowered gardens, but there's nothing old-fashioned about the prices: Hotels and restaurants should be chosen with care. Nightclubbers will be in their element here, while the resort's summer season buzzes with prestigious events, such as show jumping of horses and classic car contests. The elegant promenade, overlooking the huge beach, is lined with luxury hotels and features a casino.

㉝ From La Baule head 72 kilometers (45 miles) east, past St-Nazaire and its struggling shipyard, to **Nantes,** a tranquil, prosperous city that seems to pursue its existence without too much concern for what's going on elsewhere in France. Although Nantes is not really part of Brittany—officially it belongs to the Pays de la Loire—the dukes of Brittany were in no doubt that Nantes belonged to their domain, and the castle they built is the city's principal tourist attraction.

Numbers in the margin correspond to points of interest on the Nantes map.

㉞ The **Château des Ducs de Bretagne** is a massive, well-preserved 15th-century fortress with a neatly grassed moat. The duke responsible for building most of it was François II, who led a hedonistic existence here, surrounded by ministers, chamberlains, and an army of servants. Numerous monarchs later stayed in the castle, where, in 1598, Henri IV signed the famous Edict of Nantes advocating religious tolerance.

Within the Harnachement—a separate building inside the castle walls—you'll find the **Musée des Salorges** (Naval Museum), devoted principally to the history of seafaring; a separate section outlines the triangular trade that involved transportation of African blacks to America to be sold as slaves. As you cross the courtyard to the Grand Gouvernement wing, home to the **Musée d'Art Populaire Régional** (Regional Folk Art Museum), look for the old well, where the ducal coat of arms is entwined in a magnificent wrought-iron decoration. The Musée d'Art Populaire features an array of armor, furniture, 19th-century Breton costumes, and reconstituted interiors illustrating the former life of the Vendée region to the south. *Just off rue du Château. Admission: 15 frs., free Sun. Castle and museums open Sept.–June, Wed.–Mon. 10–noon and 2–6, closed Tues.; July–Aug., daily 10–noon and 2–6.*

㉟ Opposite the castle is the **Cathédrale St-Pierre,** one of France's latest Gothic cathedrals; building began only in 1434, well after most other medieval cathedrals had been completed. The facade is ponderous and austere, in contrast to the light, wide, elegant interior, whose vaults rise higher (120 feet) than those of Notre-Dame in Paris. In the transept, notice Michel Co-

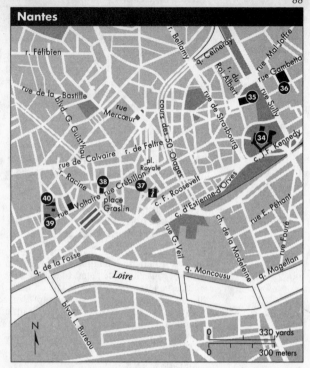

lombe's early 16th-century tomb of François II and his wife,
Marguerite de Foix, which is one of France's finest examples of
funerary sculpture. *Pl. St-Pierre.*

③⑥ Behind the cathedral, past the 15th-century Porte St-Pierre, is
the **Musée des Beaux-Arts** (Fine Arts Museum), with a fine collection of paintings from the Renaissance on, featuring works
by Jacopo Tintoretto, Georges de la Tour, Jean-Auguste In-
gres, and Gustave Courbet. *10 rue G-Clemenceau. Admission:
10 frs., free Sun. Open Wed.–Mon. 10–noon and 1–5:15.*

The cobbled streets around the castle and cathedral make up
the town's medieval sector. Across cours des 50 Otages, a broad
boulevard, is the 19th-century city. From place Royale stroll
and window-shop down busy rue Crébillon. Halfway down on
③⑦ the left is the **Passage Pommeraye,** an elegant shopping gallery
erected in 1843. At the far end of rue Crébillon is place Graslin
③⑧ and its 1783 **Grand Théâtre.**

Time Out Miniature palm trees, gleaming woodwork, colorful enamel
tiles, and painted ceilings have led to **La Cigale** (4 pl. Graslin)
being officially recognized as a *monument historique.* You can
savor its Belle Epoque ambience without spending a fortune:
The 69- and 120-franc menus are just right for a quick lunch,
although the banks of fresh oysters and the well-stacked dessert cart may tempt you to go for a leisurely meal à la carte.

Just along rue Voltaire from place Graslin is the 15th-century
③⑨ **Manoir de la Touche,** once home to the bishops of Nantes. Its
④⓪ medieval silhouette is offset by the mock-Romanesque **Palais**

Dobrée, next door, built by arts connoisseur Thomas Dobrée during the past century. Among the treasures within are miniatures, tapestries, medieval manuscripts, and enamels, while one room is devoted to the Revolutionary Wars in Vendée. *Pl. Jean V. Admission: 10 frs., free Sun. Open Wed.–Mon. 10–noon and 2–5; closed Tues.*

What to See and Do with Children

Boat trips make entertaining excursions for old and young alike. Some of the most scenic include the tour of the Golfe du Morbihan (depart from Vannes), sea jaunts from Dinard or St-Malo to the Ile de Cézembre or along the rugged coast to Cap Fréhel, cruises up the River Rance from Dinard to Dinan, and the frequent 10-minute crossings between Dinard and St-Malo. (For information on trips to the numerous islands off the Brittany shore, *see* Off the Beaten Track, below.)

These other attractions are described in the Exploring section:

Château des Ducs de Bretagne, Nantes, Tour 2.
Fougères Castle, Tour 1.
Grand Phare (Lighthouse), Belle-Ile, Tour 2.
Musée de Bretagne, Rennes, Tour 1.
Musée de la Mer, Dinard, Tour 1.
Musée de la Pêche, Concarneau, Tour 2.
Océanopolis, Brest, Tour 2.
Vitré Castle, Tour 1.

Off the Beaten Track

You may enjoy visiting the inland countryside, particularly some of the spectacular castles north of Vannes. The first of these castles, set in a wooded park 19 kilometers (12 miles) from Vannes via N166, is the Fortress of Largoët near Elven. Its 170-foot 14th-century octagonal keep is the highest in France; its walls are up to 30 feet thick. Alongside is a faithfully restored 15th-century tower. Henry Tudor was held prisoner here before his return to England and the triumphant 1485 military campaign that led to his becoming Henry VII. *Admission: 13 frs. Open Apr.–Oct., daily 9–6.*

Continue along N166 past Brignac—a round 15th-century tower is all that remains of the fortress that once stood here—to La Chapelle. The elegant, nearby château of Le Crévy houses a collection of costumes dating from 1730.

Sixteen kilometers (10 miles) northwest along D4 is Josselin, a picturesque medieval town. Josselin Castle has two faces. Overlooking the River Oust is a defensive stronghold with three stout turreted towers linked by austere, near-windowless walls. The landward facade, however, is a riot of intricate pinnacles, gables, and stone ornament, surrounded by gardens. You can visit the library, wood-paneled dining room, portrait gallery, and Grand Salon, with its ornate fireplace (only the ground floor is open to the public). *Admission: 21 frs. Open Apr.–May and Oct. 1–Nov. 15, Wed., Sat., and Sun. 2–6; June–Aug., daily 10–noon and 2–6; Sept., daily 2–6.*

Another attraction in Josselin is the 500-strong collection of old dolls displayed in the former castle stables. Many are dressed in traditional costume; most date from the 18th century, and one dates from the 17th century. *Admission: 22 frs. (separate from castle). Open May–Sept., Tues.–Sun. 10–noon and 2–6; Mar., Apr., and Oct.–mid-Nov., Wed. and weekends 10–noon and 2–6.*

The cheerful old town of **Rochefort-en-Terre**, 45 kilometers (28 miles) south of Josselin, boasts a cozy, ivory-clad 14th-century castle. The interior holds tapestries, armor, chests, and old furniture; earthenware statuettes; and paintings by Alfred and Trafford Klots, American artists who lived here and restored the castle. *Admission: 12 frs. Open Apr.–May, weekends 10–12:30 and 2–6:30; June–Sept., daily 10–12:30 and 2–6:30.*

In addition to Belle-Ile (*see* Exploring, above), several other islands off the Brittany coast, none more than a few miles long, can also be visited. Take your pick from these:

Batz, with its tame landscape and sandy beaches. *Frequent daily crossings from Roscoff. Journey time: 15 minutes.*

Ouessant, whose melancholy scenery surrounds an ornithological research center for bird enthusiasts. *Crossings daily except Tues. from Brest. Journey time: 90 minutes.*

Molène, where relics of shipwrecks are on display at the old presbytery. *Crossings daily except Tues. from Brest. Journey time: 90 minutes.*

Sein, featuring narrow streets and a spectacular setting off the rugged Pointe de Raz. *Crossings daily except Wed. from Audierne.*

Glénan Archipelago, a string of eight uninhabited islands and dozens of rocks and islets. *Frequent crossings in summer from Concarneau.*

Groix, with its cliffs and sandy beaches. *Daily crossings from Lorient. Journey time: 45 minutes.*

Houat, highlighted by creeks, dunes, and beaches. *Daily crossings from Quiberon and Vannes. Journey time: 60 minutes.*

Hoëdic, a granite outcrop with just 126 inhabitants. *Daily crossings from Quiberon. Journey time: 90 minutes.*

Shopping

Folk Costumes and Textiles
When it comes to distinctive Breton folk costumes, **Quimper** is the best place to look. The streets around the cathedral (especially **rue du Parc**) are full of shops, several selling the woolen goods (notably thick marine sweaters) in which the region also specializes. Addresses for good textiles in **Rennes** are **Tidreiz** (pl. du Palais) and **Au Roy d'Ys** (29 blvd. de Magenta).

Gift Ideas
The commercial quarter of **Nantes** stretches from place Royale to place Graslin. For antiques, try **Cibot** (7 rue Voltaire). Don't miss chocolate specialist **Georges Gautier** (9 rue de la Fosse), with his *Muscadets Nantais*—grapes dipped in brandy and covered with chocolate. **Quimper** is best known for its faïence—hand-painted earthenware—which can be bought at the **Kéraluc Faiencerie** (14 rue de la Troménie on the Bénodet road) or at **Henriot** (12 pl. St-Corentin). Keep an eye out for such typical Breton products as woven or embroidered cloth, brass and wooden goods, puppets, dolls, and locally designed jewelry.

Markets
Among Brittany's most colorful markets are the ones held at Talensac in **Nantes** and in the streets of old **St-Malo** (Tuesday and Friday only). The most interesting street for arts and

crafts is the cobbled, sloping **rue de Jerzual** in **Dinan,** whose medieval houses contain an assortment of wood-carvers, jewelers, leather workers, glass specialists, and silk painters.

Sports and Fitness

Beaches and Water Sports From St-Malo to Brest as far as the Côte d'Emeraude, then south to Nantes, the Brittany coast has any number of clean sandy **beaches**—the best are found at Dinard, Perros-Guirec, Trégastel-Plage, Douarnenez, Carnac, and Baule. Resorts offer numerous sports facilities ranging from **underwater diving** and **spearfishing** to **canoeing** and **sandsailing** (at St-Pierre Quiberon). To rent **sailboats,** try StMalo (tel. 99–82–00–78), Carnac (tel. 97–52–02–41), Douarnenez (**Iroise Nautique,** tel. 98–74–29–38), Dinard (**Yacht Club,** tel. 99–46–14–32), or Morlaix (**Loisirs 3000,** tel. 98–88–27–30).

Windsurfing possibilities include Carnac (boards can be rented from **De Petigny** at 90 rte. du Pô, tel. 97–52–02–41), the **Wishbone Club** in Dinard (Pont d'Emeraude), and the **Centre Nautique** in Brest (tel. 98–02–11–93). **Waterskiers** can try Concarneau (tel. 98–97–41–03). Among the region's **swimming pools** are those at Brest, Concarneau, Douarnenez, Morlaix, Quimper, Dinard, and St-Malo.

Bicycling Bikes can be rented at the train stations in Brest (tel. 98–44–21–55), Morlaix (tel. 98–88–60–47), and Quimper (tel. 98–80–50–50); in St-Malo, from **Diazo** (tel. 99–40–31–63); in Dol, from **Cycles Nicole** (tel. 99–48–03–20); or at Carnac (tel. 97–52–02–33) and Dinard (**Duval Cycles,** tel. 99–46–19–63).

Horseback Riding Riding stables include St-Malo (**Société Hippique,** tel. 99–81–20–34), Dinan (tel. 96–27–14–62), Carnac (**Centre Equestre des Menhirs,** tel. 97–55–73–45), and Dinard (**Centre Equestre de la Cote d'Emeraude,** tel. 99–46–23–57).

Dining and Lodging

Dining

Not surprisingly, Breton cuisine is dominated by fish and seafood. Shrimp, crayfish, crabs, oysters, and scallops are found throughout the region, but the linchpin of Breton menus is often lobster, prepared in sauce or cream or grilled. Popular meats include ham and lamb, frequently served with kidney beans. Fried eel is a traditional dish in the Nantes district. Brittany is particularly famous for its crepes, served with both sweet and savory fillings. Accompanied by a glass of local cider, they make an ideal basis for a light, inexpensive meal.

Highly recommended restaurants are indicated by a star ★.

Category	Cost*
Very Expensive	over 350 francs
Expensive	200–350 francs

| Moderate | 100–200 francs |
| Inexpensive | under 100 francs |

*per person for a three-course meal, including tax (18.6%) and
tip but not wine*

Lodging

Brittany's economy is heavily dependent on tourism, and its
hotel infrastructure is correspondingly dense. Recent TGV
(high-speed train) links make the area easily accessible from
Paris, bringing larger crowds in the summer, so it is always
best to make reservations far in advance. The charm of many of
the region's lodging places is that they are family-run and can
be quite small, encouraging the friendly, personal service for
which the Bretons are known. Brittany also has a growing
number of luxury hotels and beautiful old châteaus converted
into lodgings, many of which offer thalassatherapy (sea water)
treatments, sporting facilities, swimming, and top-notch dining in elegant, natural settings. Dinard, on the English Channel, and La Baule, on the Atlantic, are the two most exclusive
resorts; Quiberon, also on the Atlantic, is more run down. All
three areas offer larger hotels and a greater choice of restaurants.

Highly recommended hotels are indicated by a star ★.

Category	Cost*
Very Expensive	over 750 francs
Expensive	350–750 francs
Moderate	200–350 francs
Inexpensive	under 200 francs

*All prices are for a standard double room for two, including
tax (18.6%) and service charge.*

Audierne
Dining and Lodging
★

Le Goyen. This beautiful, cozy inn sits at the edge of the bustling fishing port of Audierne. In the early morning you can
lounge on the terrace of one of the charming flower-print-and-
chintz–decorated double rooms and watch the activity below,
or sip an aperitif on your aerie as the village winds down late in
the day. Choose a table with a port view in the restaurant,
where the specialties are roast sea bass and lobster brought
from quay to kitchen that morning. *Portside, tel. 98–70–08–88.
29 rooms with bath. Reservations advised. Jacket required in
dining room. MC, V. Closed Jan.–Feb. and Mon. off-season.
Expensive.*

La Baule
Dining

La Marcaderie. This warm, yellow-walled restaurant has replaced L'Espadon (now closed) as the best in town, helped by
the cheerful welcome of Jean-Luc Girard and his wife. Potato
and scampi tart or scallops in endive figure on the inventive
menu. *5 av. d'Agen, tel. 40–24–03–12. Reservations required.
Jacket and tie required. AE, MC, V. Closed Mon., Sun. evening, and Jan. Moderate–Expensive.*
La Pergola. The inventive finesse of its haute cuisine and the
warmth of its welcome have given La Pergola a substantial reputation. The restaurant is conveniently situated in the center of

La Baule, next to the casino and a stone's throw from the beach. Meat and fish are prepared with aplomb in a variety of subtle sauces. There is a set menu that's moderately priced, but you'll wind up in the expensive range if you eat à la carte. *147 av. des Lilas, tel. 40–24–57–61. Reservations advised. Jacket required. MC, V. Closed for lunch Mon., Wed., and Fri. Moderate.*

Lodging **Concorde.** This establishment numbers among the least expensive good hotels in pricey La Baule. It's calm, comfortable, recently modernized, and close to the beach (ask for a room with a sea view). There's no restaurant. *1 av. de la Concorde, 44500, tel. 40–60–23–09. 47 rooms with bath or shower. Closed Oct.–Easter. Moderate.*

Belle-Ile **La Forge.** A sure bet for lunch or dinner, La Forge specializes in
Dining traditional cuisine, based on seafood and fish, at affordable prices. Old wooden beams and remnants of the building's original purpose—blacksmithing—contribute to the pleasant, rustic atmosphere. *Rte. de Port-Goulphar, Bangor, tel. 91–31–51–76. Reservations required in summer. Dress: casual. AE, DC, MC, V. Closed Wed. and Jan.–Feb. Moderate.*

Cancale **Bricourt.** The picturesque fishing village of Cancale, 13 kilome-
Dining ters (8 miles) east of St-Malo via D355, is the setting for what is
★ probably one of the region's best restaurants. The highly rated young chef, Olivier Roellinger, created the restaurant in the house in which he grew up, and the murals, stone fireplaces, and worn tiles create an atmosphere that is both appetizing and cozy. Local seafood dishes are his specialty, but his are seasoned with exotic spices more indigenous to Indonesia than to the côte d'Emeraude, as this strip of the Brittany coast is known. Desserts are not to be missed. *1 rue Duguesclin, tel. 99–89–64–76. Reservations advised. Jacket required. AE, DC, MC, V. Closed Tues. and Wed. in winter, Tues. only in July and Aug., and Jan.–Mar. Expensive.*

Concarneau **Le Chalut.** In a town dominated by the fishing industry, the
Dining best bet for an inexpensive lunch is where the fishermen and dockworkers themselves might go. A simple, quayside restaurant, Le Chalut offers hearty grillades as well as light salads with generous portions of cold seafood. *20 quai Carnot, tel. 98–97–02–12. Reservations not necessary. Dress: casual. AE, MC, V. Closed Sun. Inexpensive.*

Dinan **Relais des Corsaires.** The old hilltop town of Dinan is full of res-
Dining taurants and crepe houses, but we suggest that you wander down to the old port on the banks of the Rance to dine at this spot, quaintly named after the pirates who apparently raided the wharves of Dinan. The mid-range fixed-price menu provides an ample four-course meal, with alternative menus at higher and lower prices. The costlier à la carte choices are not as good for the money. There are two separate, oak-beamed dining rooms; the lush main room with aquarium and attentive, rather unctuous service, communicates by way of a hatch with a smaller room with an impressively long bar, patrolled by Madame Ternisien, the attractive *patronne* who likes to give herself the airs and graces of a grande dame. *7 rue du Quai, tel. 96–39–40–17. Reservations accepted. Dress: casual. AE, DC, MC, V. Inexpensive.*

Dining and Lodging **D'Avagour.** This hotel is splendidly situated opposite Dinan Castle's Tour du Connétable and has its own flower garden to boot; most of the cozy guest rooms look out onto either the garden or the castle. You can be sure of a warm welcome from the affable owner, Madame Quinton. The hotel attracts numerous foreign guests—American, English, and Italian, in particular. The restaurant offers traditional cuisine (shellfish, duck, apple tart) at reasonable prices (even considering that they go up dramatically from lunch to dinner), plus the chance to dine in the garden in warm weather. *1 pl. du Champ-Clos, 22100, tel. 96–39–07–49. 27 rooms with bath. Facilities: restaurant, garden. AE, DC, MC, V. Moderate.*

Dinard
Dining and Lodging

La Vallée. Prices at this traditional late-19th-century hotel vary according to the room. The best have a sea view: The Clair de Lune Promenade and Prieuré Beach are within shouting distance. The hotel itself is decorated in a stockily elegant fin-de-siècle style, with an authentic French feel. The restaurant's seafood comes on the moderate and expensive menus. *6 av. George-V, 35800, tel. 99–46–94–00. 26 rooms with bath. Facilities: restaurant. V. Closed mid-Nov.–mid-Dec., second half of Jan.; restaurant closed Tues. Oct.–Apr. Moderate.*

Dol-de-Bretagne
Dining and Lodging

Logis de la Bresche Arthur. With its crisp outlines, white walls, and ample glass frontage, the hotel may not be quite as historic as it sounds, but it remains the coziest place in Dol in which to spend a night. The rooms are functional; local character is reserved for the restaurant, where smoked salmon, seafish, and home-prepared foie gras top the menu. *36 blvd. Deminiac, 35120, tel. 99–48–01–44. 24 rooms with bath. Facilities: restaurant. AE, DC, MC, V. Moderate.*

Morlaix
Dining and Lodging
★

Europe. Occupying an old building in the town center, the Europe is easily the best hotel in town, with simple, modernized guest rooms. Its restaurant (low-cost fixed-price menus, higher à la carte) provides an exuberant welcome, sumptuous many-mirrored decor, and some exciting recipes featuring lobster, warm oysters, and smoked salmon. *1 rue d'Aiguillon, 29210, tel. 98–62–11–99. 67 rooms, some with bath. Facilities: restaurant. AE, DC, MC, V. Inexpensive–Moderate.*

Nantes
Dining
★

Colvert. This small, modern bistro serves interesting dishes based on seafood or game, according to season. Chef Didier Macoin is an expert at devising original sauces (lentils and honey to accompany roast pigeon), and the inexpensive lunchtime menu, including aperitif, is an excellent value. *14 rue Armand-Brossard, tel. 40–48–20–02. Reservations advised. Dress: casual. MC, V. Closed Sat. lunch, Sun., and Sept. Moderate.*

Mon Rêve. Fine food and a delectable parkland setting are offered at this cozy little restaurant about 8 kilometers (5 miles) east of town. Chef Gérard Ryngel concocts elegantly inventive regional fare (the duck or rabbit in muscadet are good choices), while his wife, Cécile, presides over the dining room with aplomb. *Rte. des Bords de Loire, Basse-Goulaine, tel. 40–03–55–50. Reservations advised. Dress: casual. AE, DC, MC, V. Closed 2 weeks in Feb., and Wed. during Oct.–Mar. Moderate.*

Lodging

Hotel Graslin. This hotel is distinctly French: modest, cozy, and comfortable and run with discreet efficiency by the couple who own it. Monsieur and Madame Cassard also manage to keep their prices reasonable. *1 rue Piron, tel. 40–69–72–91. 47 rooms with bath. AE, DC, MC, V. Inexpensive.*

Pont-Aven
Dining

La Taupinière. Situated 16 kilometers (10 miles) from Concarneau along D783 on the outskirts of Pont-Aven, this roadside inn has an attractive garden. The food doesn't come cheap, but, then, chef Guy Guilloux doesn't dabble in mediocrity. Fish, crab, crayfish, and Breton ham (perhaps grilled over the large, open fire) are the bases of his inventions, while his wine cellar is renowned. *Rte. de Concarneau, tel. 98–06–03–12. Reservations required. Jacket required. MC, V. Closed Mon. dinner, Tues., and mid-Sept.–mid-Oct. Expensive.*

Dining and Lodging **Moulin de Rosmadec.** This faithfully restored old mill sits in the middle of the rushing, rocky, Aven River. There are only a handful of newly appointed rooms attached to the original establishment, but in each of these you'll fall asleep to the sound of water gently spilling over the stones beneath your window. The restaurant is one of the best in France, serving such seafood dishes as lobster- and langoustine-stuffed ravioli in a rustic dining room decorated with sturdy Breton furnishings. *Town center, tel. 98–06–00–22. 4 rooms with bath. Reservations required. Jacket required in dining room. MC, V. Closed Sun. evening and Wed. mid-Sept.–mid-June and Feb. and Oct. 15–31. Expensive.*

Rennes **Palais.** The best, though not the most expensive, restaurant in
Dining Rennes must thank its highly inventive team of young chefs for
★ its considerable reputation. Specialties include roast rabbit and, during winter, fried oysters in crab sauce. The lightish cuisine varies according to season and is offered via two menus. The decor is sharp-edged contemporary, the site conveniently central. *6 pl. du Parlement de Bretagne, tel. 99–79–45–01. Dinner reservations required. Jacket required. AE, DC, MC, V. Closed Sun. dinner, Mon., and Aug. Moderate.*

★ **Le Grain de Sable.** Situated at the bottom of rue des Dames leading to the cathedral is a thoroughly unusual restaurant. Plants, candelabra, faded photographs, and a settee in the middle of the dining room create an ambience that escapes tackiness only by sheer eccentricity (a rocking horse sways in one corner). The cuisine is equally offbeat; expect garlic puree or endive with melted cheese to accompany the grilled meats that dominate the menu. Piped music warbles from opera to Louis Armstrong as the playful waitresses receive noisy reprimands from Hervé in the kitchen. *2 rue des Dames, tel. 99–30–78–18. Reservations advised. Dress: casual. MC, V. Closed Sun., Mon. dinner. Inexpensive.*

Lodging **Central.** This stately, late-19th-century hotel lives up to its name and sits close to Rennes Cathedral. The individually decorated guest rooms look out over the street or courtyard; the latter quieter. English-speaking guests are frequent. There's no restaurant. *6 rue Lanjuinais, 35000, tel. 99–79–12–36. 43 rooms, most with bath. AE, DC, MC, V. Moderate.*

Angélina. This little charmer wins on sheer unpretentiousness: friendly welcome, clean rooms, robust breakfasts, and windows double-glazed to keep out the noise (it is on Rennes's principal boulevard, within a five-minute walk of the old town). Don't be put off by the fact that the hotel begins on the third floor of an ordinary-looking street block. *1 quai Lamennais, 35100, tel. 99–79–29–66. 26 rooms, with shower or bath. AE, DC, MC, V. Inexpensive.*

Riec-sur-Belon **Chez Jacky.** This is France's answer to an all-you-can-eat menu;
Dining whatever you eat here is as fresh as it can possibly be. All the fare comes directly from the Belon River, the source of some of the country's best oysters. *Rive Droite, tel. 98–06–90–32. Res-*

ervations advised. *Dress: casual. MC, V. Closed Mon. Oct.–Mar. Inexpensive.*

Ste-Anne-la-Palud **Hotel de la Plage.** At what seems like the end of the earth (it is
Dining and Lodging indeed the end of Brittany), this former private house sits nestled in a cove on a quiet strip of smooth, sandy beach. Some of the comfortably furnished rooms face the sea and are afforded magnificent sunsets; others look out onto rolling dunes carpeted with scrub pines. Part of the Relais & Chateaux group, the hotel is situated in an area that is great for long, restorative walks—the sort that work up an appetite for the seafood specialties served in the hotel's highly rated restaurant. *29127 Plonevez-Porzay, tel. 98–92–50–12. 26 rooms with bath. Facilities: tennis courts, private beach. Reservations required. Jacket required. AE, DC, MC, V. Closed Nov.–Mar. Expensive.*

St-Malo **Café de la Bourse.** Wherever you search for a restaurant in the
Dining old town of St-Malo, you will feel you are being hemmed into an overcommercialized tourist trap. This restaurant, where prawns and oysters are downed by the shovel, is no exception. However, though its wooden seats and some tacky navigational paraphernalia—ships' wheels and posters of grizzled old sea dogs—are hardly artistic, the large, L-shaped dining room makes amends with genuinely friendly service and a seafood platter for two that includes at least three tanklike crabs, plus an army of cockles, whelks, and periwinkles. *1 rue de Dinan, tel. 99–56–47–17. Reservations accepted. Dress: casual. AE, V. Inexpensive–Moderate.*

Lodging **La Digue.** Many of the rooms and the breakfast terrace at this hotel face the sea, offering magnificent views over St-Malo's long beach. The largest and most luxurious apartments are pricey, but many others are quite reasonably priced. A bar and *salon de thé* (tearoom) add to the hotel's attractions. *49 chaussée du Sillon, 35400, tel. 99–56–09–26. 53 rooms, some with bath. Facilities: bar, tearoom. AE, V. Closed mid-Nov.–mid-Mar. Moderate–Expensive.*
Jean-Bart. This clean, quiet hotel next to the ramparts, whose decor makes liberal use of cool blue, bears the stamp of diligent renovation: The beds are comfortable, the bathrooms shiny-modern, but the rooms are somewhat small. (Some offer sea views.) *12 rue de Chartres, 35400, tel. 99–40–33–88. 17 rooms, most with bath. MC, V. Closed mid-Nov.–mid-Feb. Moderate.*

Vannes **Lys.** Intricate, nouvelle cuisine, based on fresh local produce,
Dining makes this restaurant a pleasant dinner spot, close to the agreeable Promenade de la Garenne. The setting, in a late-18th-century Louis XVI style, is at its best by candlelight, with piano music in the background. *51 rue du Maréchal-Leclerc, tel. 97–47–29–30. Reservations required. Jacket and tie required. AE, DC, MC, V. Closed Mon., mid-Nov.–mid-Dec., and Sun. dinner. Moderate.*

Lodging **Image Ste-Anne.** This charming hotel is housed in a suitably old, rustic building in the center of historic Vannes. The warm welcome and comfortable guest rooms make the price of a night here seem more than acceptable, as a varied foreign clientele has realized. Mussels, sole in cider, and duck are featured on the restaurant's menus; set menus are all very reasonably priced. *8 pl. de la Libération, 56000, tel. 97–63–27–36. 35* rooms with bath or shower. Facilities: restaurant. MC, V. Restaurant closed Sun. dinner, Nov.–Mar. Moderate.

Vitré
Lodging
Chêne Vert. Vitré is badly placed in the hotel stakes, but we suggest this establishment, which is conveniently accessible from the road (D857, which links Rennes and Laval), just opposite the train station and a 10-minute stroll through cobbled streets from Vitré Castle. It is the epitome of a French provincial hotel: creaky stairs, fraying carpets, oversoft mattresses, and less-than-enthusiastic service—all, including a copious dinner, for next to nothing. Look carefully, however, and you will notice some intriguing touches—an enormous model ship on the second floor, for example, or the zinc-plated walls that submerge the dining room in art deco/ocean-liner pastiche. *2 pl. de la Gare, 35500, tel. 99–75–00–58. 22 rooms, a few with bath. Closed mid-Sept.–mid-Oct.; restaurant closed Fri. dinner and Sat., Oct.–May. Inexpensive.*

The Arts and Nightlife

The Arts

Pardons—the numerous traditional religious parades-cum-pilgrimages that invariably showcase age-old local costumes—are the backbone of Breton culture. There are further manifestations of local folklore, often including dancers and folk singers, at the various Celtic festivals held in summer, of which the **Festival de Cornouaille** in Quimper (late July) is the biggest.

Theater
The region's principal theaters are the **Théâtre de la Ville** in Rennes (pl. de la Mairie, tel. 99–28–55–87), the **Théâtre Châteaubriand** in St-Malo (6 rue Groult-St-Georges, tel. 99–40–98–05), and the **Théâtre Graslin** in Nantes (rue Scribe, tel. 40–69–77–18).

Concerts
Of particular note is the **Festival de la Musique Sacrée** (sacred music) held in St-Malo in August.

Nightlife

Bars and Nightclubs
In Saint-Malo: **Le Faubourg** (7 rue St-Thomas), **La Selle** (24 rue Ste-Barbe), or **La Belle Epoque** (11 rue de Dinan). In Rennes, try **Le Pym's** (27 pl. du Colombier); in Nantes, the piano bar **Le Tie Break** (1 rue des Petites-Ecuries); and in Brest, **Le Stendhal** (18 rue Colbert).

Jazz Clubs
Two regional jazz venues are the **Cave du Louisiane** in St-Malo (14 rue des Cordiers) and the **Pub Univers** in Nantes (16 rue J. J. Rousseau).

Discos
Les Chandelles in Carnac (av. de l'Atlantique) attracts a cosmopolitan crowd and enjoys a reputation as one of the country's leading discos. You could also try **L'Escalier** in St-Malo (rue du Tour-du-Bonheur) or **L'Espace** in Rennes (45 blvd. de la Tour d'Auvergne).

Casinos
There are casinos in **Dinard** (tel. 99–46–15–71), **Fréhel** (tel. 96–41–49–05), **Perros-Guirec** (tel. 96–23–20–51), **Quiberon** (tel. 97–50–23–57), and **La Baule** (tel. 40–60–20–23).

For Singles
Le Batchi in Rennes (34 rue Vasselot) and **L'Interdit** in Nantes (14 rue Menou) cater to men only.

Conversion Tables

Distance

Kilometers/Miles To change kilometers to miles, multiply kilometers by .621
To change miles to kilometers, multiply miles by 1.61

Km to Mi	Mi to Km
1 = .62	1 = 1.6
2 = 1.2	2 = 3.2
3 = 1.9	3 = 4.8
4 = 2.5	4 = 6.4
5 = 3.1	5 = 8.1
6 = 3.7	6 = 9.7
7 = 4.3	7 = 11.3
8 = 5.0	8 = 12.9
9 = 5.6	9 = 14.5

Meters/Feet To change meters to feet, multiply meters by 3.28
To change feet to meters, multiply feet by .305

Meters to Feet	Feet to Meters
1 = 3.3	1 = .31
2 = 6.6	2 = .61
3 = 9.8	3 = .92
4 = 13.1	4 = 1.2
5 = 16.4	5 = 1.5
6 = 19.7	6 = 1.8
7 = 23.0	7 = 2.1
8 = 26.2	8 = 2.4
9 = 29.5	9 = 2.7

Weight

Kilograms/Pounds To change kilograms to pounds, multiply by 2.20
To change pounds to kilograms, multiply by .453

Kilos to Pounds	Pounds to Kilos
1 = 2.2	1 = .45
2 = 4.4	2 = .91
3 = 6.6	3 = 1.4
4 = 8.8	4 = 1.8
5 = 11.0	5 = 2.3

6 = 13.2	6 = 2.7
7 = 15.4	7 = 3.2
8 = 17.6	8 = 3.6
9 = 19.8	9 = 4.1

Grams/Ounces To change grams to ounces, multiply grams by .035
To change ounces to grams, multiply ounces by 28.4

Grams to Ounces	Ounces to Grams
1 = .04	1 = 28
2 = .07	2 = 57
3 = .11	3 = 85
4 = .14	4 = 114
5 = .18	5 = 142
6 = .21	6 = 170
7 = .25	7 = 199
8 = .28	8 = 227
9 = .32	9 = 256

Liquid Volume

Liters/U.S. Gallons To change liters to U.S. gallons, multiply liters by .264
To change U.S. gallons to liters, multiply gallons by 3.79

Liters to U.S. Gallons	U.S. Gallons to Liters
1 = .26	1 = 3.8
2 = .53	2 = 7.6
3 = .79	3 = 11.4
4 = 1.1	4 = 15.2
5 = 1.3	5 = 19.0
6 = 1.6	6 = 22.7
7 = 1.8	7 = 26.5
8 = 2.1	8 = 30.3
9 = 2.4	9 = 34.1

Clothing Sizes

Men To change American suit sizes to French suit sizes, add 10 to
Suits the American suit size.

To change French suit sizes to American suit sizes, subtract 10
from the French suit size.

U.S.	36	38	40	42	44	46	48
French	46	48	50	52	54	56	58

Shirts To change American shirt sizes to French shirt sizes, multiply the American shirt size by 2 and add 8.

To change French shirt sizes to American shirt sizes, subtract 8 from the French shirt size and divide by 2.

U.S.	14	14½	15	15½	16	16½	17	17½
French	36	37	38	39	40	41	42	43

Shoes French shoe sizes vary in their relation to American shoe sizes.

U.S.	6½	7	8	9	10	10½	11
French	39	40	41	42	43	44	45

Women
Dresses and Coats To change U.S. dress/coat sizes to French dress/coat sizes, add 28 to the U.S. dress/coat size.

To change French dress/coat sizes to U.S. dress/coat sizes, subtract 28 from the French dress/coat size.

U.S.	4	6	8	10	12	14	16
French	32	34	36	38	40	42	44

Blouses and Sweaters To change U.S. blouse/sweater sizes to French blouse/sweater sizes, add 8 to the U.S. blouse/sweater size.

To change French blouse/sweater sizes to U.S. blouse/sweater sizes, subtract 8 from the French blouse/sweater size.

U.S.	30	32	34	36	38	40	42
French	38	40	42	44	46	48	50

Shoes To change U.S. shoe sizes to French shoe sizes, add 32 to the U.S. shoe size.

To change French shoe sizes to U.S. shoe sizes, subtract 32 from the French shoe size.

U.S.	4	5	6	7	8	9	10
French	36	37	38	39	40	41	42

French Vocabulary

Words and Phrases

	English	French	Pronunciation
Basics	Yes/no	Oui/non	wee/no
	Please	S'il vous plaît	seel voo play
	Thank you	Merci	mare-**see**
	You're welcome	De rien	deh ree-**en**
	Excuse me, sorry	Pardon	pahr-**doan**
	Sorry!	Désolé(e)	day-zoh-**lay**
	Good morning/ afternoon	Bonjour	bone-**joor**
	Good evening	Bonsoir	bone-**swar**
	Goodbye	Au revoir	o ruh-**vwar**
	Mr. (Sir)	Monsieur	mih-see-**oor**
	Mrs. (Ma'am)	Madame	ma-dam
	Miss	Mademoiselle	mad-mwa-**zel**
	Pleased to meet you	Enchanté(e)	on-shahn-**tay**
	How are you?	Comment allez-vous?	ko-men-tahl-ay-**voo**
Numbers	one	un	un
	two	deux	dew
	three	trois	twa
	four	quatre	**cat**-ruh
	five	cinq	sank
	six	six	seess
	seven	sept	set
	eight	huit	wheat
	nine	neuf	nuf
	ten	dix	deess
	eleven	onze	owns
	twelve	douze	dooz
	thirteen	treize	trays
	fourteen	quatorze	ka-torz
	fifteen	quinze	cans
	sixteen	seize	sez
	seventeen	dix-sept	deess-**set**
	eighteen	dix-huit	deess-**wheat**
	nineteen	dix-neuf	deess-**nuf**
	twenty	vingt	vant
	twenty-one	vingt-et-un	vant-ay-**un**
	thirty	trente	trahnt
	forty	quarante	ka-**rahnt**
	fifty	cinquante	sang-**kahnt**
	sixty	soixante	swa-**sahnt**
	seventy	soixante-dix	swa-sahnt-**deess**
	eighty	quatre-vingts	cat-ruh-**vant**
	ninety	quatre-vingt-dix	cat-ruh-vant-**deess**
	one-hundred	cent	sahnt
	one-thousand	mille	meel
Colors	black	noir	nwar
	blue	bleu	blu
	brown	brun/marron	brun

green	vert	vair
orange	orange	o-**ranj**
red	rouge	rouge
white	blanc	blahn
yellow	jaune	jone

Days of the Week

Sunday	dimanche	dee-**mahnsh**
Monday	lundi	lewn-**dee**
Tuesday	mardi	mar-**dee**
Wednesday	mercredi	mare-kruh-**dee**
Thursday	jeudi	juh-**dee**
Friday	vendredi	van-dra-**dee**
Saturday	samedi	sam-**dee**

Months

January	janvier	jan-**vyay**
February	février	feh-vree-**ay**
March	mars	marce
April	avril	a-**vreel**
May	mai	meh
June	juin	jwan
July	juillet	jwee-**ay**
August	août	oot
September	septembre	sep-**tahm**-bruh
October	octobre	oak-**toe**-bruh
November	novembre	no-**vahm**-bruh
December	décembre	day-**sahm**-bruh

Useful Phrases

Do you speak English?	Parlez-vous anglais?	par-lay vooz ahng-**glay**
I don't speak French	Je ne parle pas français	jeh nuh parl pah fraun-**say**
I don't understand	Je ne comprends pas	jeh nuh kohm-prahn **pah**
I understand	Je comprends	jeh kohm-**prahn**
I don't know	Je ne sais pas	jeh nuh say **pah**
I'm American/British	Je suis américain/anglais	jeh sweez a-may-ree-**can**/ahng-**glay**
What's your name?	Comment vous appelez-vous?	ko-mahn voo za-pel-ay-**voo**
My name is . . .	Je m'appelle . . .	jeh muh-**pel** . . .
What time is it?	Quelle heure est-il?	kel ur et-**il**
How?	Comment?	ko-**mahn**
When?	Quand?	kahnd
Yesterday	Hier	yair
Today	Aujourd'hui	o-zhoor-**dwee**
Tomorrow	Demain	deh-**man**
This morning/afternoon	Ce matin/cet après-midi	seh ma-**tanh**/set ah-pray-mee-**dee**
Tonight	Ce soir	seh **swar**
What?	Quoi?	kwah

What is it?	Qu'est-ce que c'est?	kess-kuh-**say**
Why?	Pourquoi?	poor-**kwa**
Who?	Qui?	kee
Where is . . .	Où est . . .	oo ay
the train station?	la gare?	la gar
the subway station?	la station de métro?	la sta-syon deh may-**tro**
the bus stop?	l'arrêt de bus?	la-ray deh **booss**
the terminal (airport)?	l'aérogare?	lay-ro-**gar**
the post office?	la poste?	la post
the bank?	la banque?	la bahnk
the . . . hotel?	l'hôtel . . . ?	low-**tel**
the . . . museum?	le musée . . . ?	leh mew-**zay**
the hospital?	l'hôpital?	low-pee-**tahl**
the elevator?	l'ascenseur?	la-sahn-**seur**
the telephone?	le téléphone?	leh te-le-**phone**
Where are the restrooms?	Où sont les toilettes?	oo son lay twah-**let**
Here/there	Ici/là	ee-**see**/la
Left/right	A gauche/à droite	a goash/a drwat
Is it near/far?	C'est près/loin?	say pray/lwan
I'd like . . .	Je voudrais . . .	jeh voo-**dray**
a room	une chambre	ewn **shahm**-bra
the key	la clé	la clay
a newspaper	un journal	un joor-**nahl**
a stamp	un timbre	un **tam**-bruh
I'd like to buy . . .	Je voudrais acheter . . .	jeh voo-**dray** ahsh-**tay**
cigarettes	des cigarettes	day see-ga-**ret**
matches	des allumettes	days a-loo-**met**
city plan	un plan de ville	un plahn de la **veel**
road map	une carte routière	ewn cart roo-tee-**air**
magazine	une revue	ewn reh-**view**
envelopes	des enveloppes	dayz ahn-veh-**lope**
writing paper	du papier à lettres	deh-pa-pee-ay a **let**-ruh
airmail writing paper	du papier avion	deh pa-pee-ay a-vee-**own**
postcard	une carte postale	ewn cart post-**al**
How much is it?	C'est combien?	say comb-bee-**en**
It's expensive/cheap	C'est cher/pas cher	say sher/pa sher
A little/a lot	Un peu/beaucoup	un puh/bo-**koo**
More/less	Plus/moins	ploo/mwa
Enough/too (much)	Assez/trop	a-**say**/tro
I am ill/sick	Je suis malade	jeh swee ma-**lahd**

Call a doctor	Appelez un docteur	a-pe-lay un dohk-**tore**
Help!	Au secours!	o say-**koor**
Stop!	Arrêtez!	a-ruh-**tay**

Dining Out

A bottle of . . .	une bouteille de . . .	ewn boo-**tay** deh
A cup of . . .	une tasse de . . .	ewn tass deh
A glass of . . .	un verre de . . .	un vair deh
Ashtray	un cendrier	un sahn-dree-**ay**
Bill/check	l'addition	la-dee-see-**own**
Bread	du pain	due pan
Breakfast	le petit déjeuner	leh pet-**ee** day-zhu-**nay**
Butter	du beurre	due bur
Cocktail/aperitif	un apéritif	un ah-pay-ree-**teef**
Dinner	le dîner	leh dee-**nay**
Fixed-price menu	le menu	leh may-**new**
Fork	une fourchette	ewn four-**shet**
I am on a diet	Je suis au régime	jeh sweez o ray-**jeem**
I am vegetarian	Je suis végétarien(ne)	jeh swee vay-jay-ta-ree-**en**
I cannot eat . . .	Je ne peux pas manger de . . .	jeh nuh puh pah mahn-**jay** deh
I'd like to order	Je voudrais commander	jeh voo-**dray** ko-mahn-**day**
I'd like . . .	Je voudrais . . .	jeh voo-**dray**
I'm hungry/thirsty	J'ai faim/soif	jay fam/swahf
Is service/the tip included?	Est-ce que le service est compris?	ess keh leh sair-veess ay comb-**pree**
It's good/bad	C'est bon/mauvais	say bon/mo-**vay**
It's hot/cold	C'est chaud/froid	say sho/frwah
Knife	un couteau	un koo-**toe**
Lunch	le déjeuner	leh day-juh-**nay**
Menu	la carte	la cart
Napkin	une serviette	ewn sair-vee-**et**
Pepper	du poivre	due **pwah**-vruh
Plate	une assiette	ewn a-see-**et**
Please give me . . .	Donnez-moi . . .	doe-nay-**mwah**
Salt	du sel	dew sell
Spoon	une cuillère	ewn kwee-**air**

| Sugar | du sucre | due **sook**-ruh |
| Wine list | la carte des vins | la cart day **van** |

Menu Guide

English	*French*
Set menu	Menu à prix fixe
Dish of the day	Plat du jour
Drink included	Boisson comprise
Local specialties	Spécialités locales
Choice of vegetable accompaniment	Garniture au choix
Made to order	Sur commande
Extra charge	Supplément/En sus
When available	Selon arrivage

Breakfast

Jam	Confiture
Croissants	Croissants
Honey	Miel
Boiled egg	Oeuf à la coque
Bacon and eggs	Oeufs au bacon
Ham and eggs	Oeufs au jambon
Fried eggs	Oeufs sur le plat
Scrambled eggs	Oeufs brouillés
(Plain) omelet	Omelette (nature)
Rolls	Petits pains

Starters

Anchovies	Anchois
Chitterling sausage	Andouille(tte)
Assorted cold cuts	Assiette anglaise
Assorted pork products	Assiette de charcuterie
Small, highly seasoned sausage	Crépinette
Mixed raw vegetable salad	Crudités
Snails	Escargots
Ham (Bayonne)	Jambon (de Bayonne)
Bologna sausage	Mortadelle
Devilled eggs	Oeufs à la diable
Liver purée blended with other meat	Pâté
Tart with a rich, creamy filling of cheese, vegetables, meat or seafood	Quiche (lorraine)
Cold sausage	Saucisson
Pâté sliced and served from an earthenware pot	Terrine
Cured dried beef	Viande séchée

Salads

Diced vegetable salad	Salade russe
Endive salad	Salade d'endives
Green salad	Salade verte
Mixed salad	Salade panachée
Tuna salad	Salade de thon

Soups

Cold leek and potato cream soup	Vichyssoise
Cream of . . .	Crème de . . .
Cream of . . .	Velouté de . . .
Hearty soup	Soupe
day's soup	*du jour*
French onion soup	à l'oignon
Provençal vegetable soup	au pistou
Light soup	Potage
mashed red beans	*condé*
shredded vegetables	julienne
potato	parmentier
Fish and seafood stew	Bouillabaisse
Seafood stew (chowder)	Bisque
Stew of meat and vegetables	Pot-au-feu

Fish and Seafood

Bass	Bar
Carp	Carpe
Clams	Palourdes
Cod	Morue
Creamed salt cod	Brandade de morue
Crab	Crabe
Crayfish	Ecrevisses
Eel	Anguille
Fish stew from Marseilles	Bourride
Fish stew in wine	Matelote
Frog's legs	Cuisses de grenouilles
Herring	Harengs
Lobster	Homard
Mackerel	Maquereau
Mussels	Moules
Octopus	Poulpe
Oysters	Huîtres
Perch	Perche
Pike	Brochet
Dublin bay prawns (scampi)	Langoustines
Red mullet	Rouget
Salmon	Saumon
Scallops in creamy sauce	Coquilles St-Jacques
Sea bream	Daurade
Shrimps	Crevettes
Sole	Sole
Squid	Calmar
Trout	Truite
Tuna	Thon
Whiting	Merlan

Methods of Preparation

Baked	Au four
Fried	Frit
Grilled	Grillé
Marinated	Mariné
Poached	Poché
Sautéed	Sauté
Smoked	Fumé
Steamed	Cuit à la vapeur

Meat

Beef	Boeuf
Beef stew with vegetables, braised in red Burgundy wine	Boeuf bourguignon
Brains	Cervelle
Chops	Côtelettes
Cutlet	Escalope
Double fillet steak	Chateaubriand
Kabob	Brochette
Kidneys	Rognons
Lamb	Agneau
Leg	Gigot
Liver	Foie
Meatballs	Boulettes de viande
Pig's feet (trotters)	Pieds de cochon
Pork	Porc
Rib	Côte
Rib or rib-eye steak	Entrecôte
Sausages	Saucisses
Sausages and cured pork served with sauerkraut	Choucroute garnie
Steak (always beef)	Steak/steack
Stew	Ragoût
T-bone steak	Côte de boeuf
Tenderloin steak	Médaillon
Tenderloin of T-bone steak	Tournedos
Tongue	Langue
Veal	Veau
Veal sweetbreads	Ris de veau

Methods of Preparation

Very rare	Bleu
Rare	Saignant
Medium	A point
Well-done	Bien cuit
Baked	Au four
Boiled	Bouilli
Braised	Braisé
Fried	Frit
Grilled	Grillé
Roast	Rôti
Sautéed	Sauté
Stewed	A l'étouffée

Game and Poultry

Chicken	Poulet
Chicken breast	Suprême de volaille
Chicken stewed in red wine	Coq au vin
Chicken stewed with vegetables	Poule au pot
Spring chicken	Poussin
Duck/duckling	Canard/caneton
Duck braised with oranges and orange liqueur	Canard à l'orange
Fattened pullet	Poularde
Fowl	Volaille
Guinea fowl/young guinea fowl	Pintade/pintadeau
Goose	Oie

Partridge/young partridge	Perdrix/perdreau
Pheasant	Faisan
Pigeon/squab	Pigeon/pigeonneau
Quail	Caille
Rabbit	Lapin
Turkey/young turkey	Dinde/dindonneau
Venison (red/roe)	Cerf/chevreuil

Vegetables

Artichoke	Artichaut
Asparagus	Asperge
Brussels sprouts	Choux de Bruxelles
Cabbage (red)	Chou (rouge)
Carrots	Carottes
Cauliflower	Chou-fleur
Eggplant	Aubergines
Endive	Endives
Leeks	Poireaux
Lettuce	Laitue
Mushrooms	Champignons
Onions	Oignons
Peas	Petits pois
Peppers	Poivrons
Radishes	Radis
Spinach	Epinards
Tomatoes	Tomates
Watercress	Cresson
Zucchini	Courgette
White kidney/French beans	Haricots blancs/verts
Casserole of stewed eggplant, onions, green peppers, and zucchini	Ratatouille

Spices and Herbs

Bay leaf	Laurier
Chervil	Cerfeuil
Garlic	Ail
Marjoram	Marjolaine
Mustard	Moutarde
Parsley	Persil
Pepper	Poivre
Rosemary	Romarin
Tarragon	Estragon
Mixture of herbs	Fines herbes

Potatoes, Rice, and Noodles

Noodles	Nouilles
Pasta	Pâtes
Potatoes	Pommes (de terre)
matchsticks	*allumettes*
mashed and deep-fried	*dauphine*
mashed with butter and egg yolks	*duchesse*
in their jackets	*en robe des champs*
french fries	*frites*
mashed	*mousseline*
boiled/steamed	*nature/vapeur*

| Rice | Riz |
| *boiled in bouillon with onions* | *pilaf* |

Sauces and Preparations

Brown butter, parsley, lemon juice	Meunière
Curry	Indienne
Egg yolks, butter, vinegar	Hollandaise
Hot pepper	Diable
Mayonnaise flavored with mustard and herbs	Tartare
Mushrooms, red wine, shallots, beef marrow	Bordelaise
Onions, tomatoes, garlic	Provençale
Pepper sauce	Poivrade
Red wine, herbs	Bourguignon
Vinegar, egg yolks, white wine, shallots, tarragon	Béarnaise
Vinegar dressing	Vinaigrette
White sauce	Béchamel
White wine, mussel broth, egg yolks	Marinière
Wine, mushrooms, onions, shallots	Chasseur
With goose or duck liver purée and truffles	Périgueux
With Madeira wine	Madère

Cheeses

Mild:	Beaufort
	Beaumont
	Belle étoile
	Boursin
	Brie
	Cantal
	Comté
	Reblochon
	St-Paulin
	Tomme de Savoie
Sharp:	Bleu de Bresse
	Camembert
	Livarot
	Fromage au marc
	Munster
	Pont-l'Évêque
	Roquefort
Swiss:	Emmenthal
	Gruyère
	Vacherin
Goat's milk:	St-Marcellin
	Crottin de Chavignol Valençay

Cheese tart	Tarte au fromage
Small cheese tart	Ramequin
Toasted ham and cheese sandwich	Croque-monsieur

Fruits and Nuts

| Almonds | Amandes |
| Apple | Pomme |

Apricot	Abricot
Banana	Banane
Blackberries	Mûres
Blackcurrants	Cassis
Blueberries	Myrtilles
Cherries	Cerises
Chestnuts	Marrons
Coconut	Noix de coco
Dates	Dattes
Dried fruit	Fruits secs
Figs	Figues
Grapefruit	Pamplemousse
Grapes green/blue	Raisin blanc/noir
Hazelnuts	Noisettes
Lemon	Citron
Melon	Melon
Orange	Orange
Peach	Pêche
Peanuts	Cacahouètes
Pear	Poire
Pineapple	Ananas
Plums	Prunes
Prunes	Pruneaux
Raisins	Raisins secs
Raspberries	Framboises
Strawberries	Fraises
Tangerine	Mandarine
Walnuts	Noix
Watermelon	Pastèque

Desserts

Apple pie	Tarte aux pommes
Baked Alaska	Omelette norvégienne
Caramel pudding	Crème caramel
Chocolate cake	Gâteau au chocolat
Chocolate pudding	Mousse au chocolat
Custard tart	Flan
Custard	Creme anglaise
Ice cream	Glace
Layer cake	Tourte
Pear with vanilla ice cream and chocolate sauce	Poire Belle Hélène
Soufflé made with orange liqueur	Soufflé au Grand-Marnier
Sundae	Coupe (glacée)
Water ice	Sorbet
Whipped cream	Crème Chantilly
Creamy dessert of egg yolks, wine, sugar, and flavoring	Sabayon
Puff pastry filled with whipped cream or custard	Profiterole

Index

Personal Itinerary

Departure *Date*

Time

Transportation

Arrival *Date*   *Time*

Departure *Date*   *Time*

Transportation

Accommodations

Arrival *Date*   *Time*

Departure *Date*   *Time*

Transportation

Accommodations

Arrival *Date*   *Time*

Departure *Date*   *Time*

Transportation

Accommodations

Personal Itinerary

Arrival *Date*   *Time*

Departure *Date*   *Time*

Transportation

Accommodations

Arrival *Date*   *Time*

Departure *Date*   *Time*

Transportation

Accommodations

Arrival *Date*   *Time*

Departure *Date*   *Time*

Transportation

Accommodations

Arrival *Date*   *Time*

Departure *Date*   *Time*

Transportation

Accommodations

Personal Itinerary

Arrival *Date*   *Time*

Departure *Date*   *Time*

Transportation

Accommodations

Arrival *Date*   *Time*

Departure *Date*   *Time*

Transportation

Accommodations

Arrival *Date*   *Time*

Departure *Date*   *Time*

Transportation

Accommodations

Arrival *Date*   *Time*

Departure *Date*   *Time*

Transportation

Accommodations

Personal Itinerary

Arrival *Date*   *Time*

Departure *Date*   *Time*

Transportation

Accommodations

Arrival *Date*   *Time*

Departure *Date*   *Time*

Transportation

Accommodations

Arrival *Date*   *Time*

Departure *Date*   *Time*

Transportation

Accommodations

Arrival *Date*   *Time*

Departure *Date*   *Time*

Transportation

Accommodations

Personal Itinerary

Arrival *Date* *Time*

Departure *Date* *Time*

Transportation

Accommodations

Arrival *Date* *Time*

Departure *Date* *Time*

Transportation

Accommodations

Arrival *Date* *Time*

Departure *Date* *Time*

Transportation

Accommodations

Arrival *Date* *Time*

Departure *Date* *Time*

Transportation

Accommodations

Personal Itinerary

Arrival   *Date*   *Time*

Departure   *Date*   *Time*

Transportation

Accommodations

Arrival   *Date*   *Time*

Departure   *Date*   *Time*

Transportation

Accommodations

Arrival   *Date*   *Time*

Departure   *Date*   *Time*

Transportation

Accommodations

Arrival   *Date*   *Time*

Departure   *Date*   *Time*

Transportation

Accommodations

Addresses

Name	*Name*
Address	*Address*
Telephone	*Telephone*
Name	*Name*
Address	*Address*
Telephone	*Telephone*
Name	*Name*
Address	*Address*
Telephone	*Telephone*
Name	*Name*
Address	*Address*
Telephone	*Telephone*
Name	*Name*
Address	*Address*
Telephone	*Telephone*
Name	*Name*
Address	*Address*
Telephone	*Telephone*
Name	*Name*
Address	*Address*
Telephone	*Telephone*
Name	*Name*
Address	*Address*
Telephone	*Telephone*

Addresses

Name	*Name*
Address	*Address*
Telephone	*Telephone*
Name	*Name*
Address	*Address*
Telephone	*Telephone*
Name	*Name*
Address	*Address*
Telephone	*Telephone*
Name	*Name*
Address	*Address*
Telephone	*Telephone*
Name	*Name*
Address	*Address*
Telephone	*Telephone*
Name	*Name*
Address	*Address*
Telephone	*Telephone*
Name	*Name*
Address	*Address*
Telephone	*Telephone*
Name	*Name*
Address	*Address*
Telephone	*Telephone*

Addresses

Name	*Name*
Address	*Address*
Telephone	*Telephone*
Name	*Name*
Address	*Address*
Telephone	*Telephone*
Name	*Name*
Address	*Address*
Telephone	*Telephone*
Name	*Name*
Address	*Address*
Telephone	*Telephone*
Name	*Name*
Address	*Address*
Telephone	*Telephone*
Name	*Name*
Address	*Address*
Telephone	*Telephone*
Name	*Name*
Address	*Address*
Telephone	*Telephone*
Name	*Name*
Address	*Address*
Telephone	*Telephone*

Fodor's Travel Guides

U.S. Guides

Alaska

Arizona

Boston

California

Cape Cod, Martha's
Vineyard, Nantucket

The Carolinas & the
Georgia Coast

Chicago

Disney World & the
Orlando Area

Florida

Hawaii

Las Vegas, Reno,
Tahoe

Los Angeles

Maine, Vermont,
New Hampshire

Maui

Miami & the Keys

New England

New Orleans

New York City

Pacific North Coast

Philadelphia & the
Pennsylvania Dutch
Country

San Diego

San Francisco

Santa Fe, Taos,
Albuquerque

Seattle & Vancouver

The South

The U.S. & British
Virgin Islands

The Upper Great
Lakes Region

USA

Vacations in New York
State

Vacations on the
Jersey Shore

Virginia & Maryland

Waikiki

Washington, D.C.

Foreign Guides

Acapulco, Ixtapa,
Zihuatanejo

Australia & New
Zealand

Austria

The Bahamas

Baja & Mexico's
Pacific Coast Resorts

Barbados

Berlin

Bermuda

Brazil

Budapest

Budget Europe

Canada

Cancun, Cozumel,
Yucatan Penisula

Caribbean

Central America

China

Costa Rica, Belize,
Guatemala

Czechoslovakia

Eastern Europe

Egypt

Euro Disney

Europe

Europe's Great Cities

France

Germany

Great Britain

Greece

The Himalayan
Countries

Hong Kong

India

Ireland

Israel

Italy

Italy's Great Cities

Japan

Kenya & Tanzania

Korea

London

Madrid & Barcelona

Mexico

Montreal &
Quebec City

Morocco

The Netherlands
Belgium &
Luxembourg

New Zealand

Norway

Nova Scotia, Prince
Edward Island &
New Brunswick

Paris

Portugal

Rome

Russia & the Baltic
Countries

Scandinavia

Scotland

Singapore

South America

Southeast Asia

South Pacific

Spain

Sweden

Switzerland

Thailand

Tokyo

Toronto

Turkey

Vienna & the Danube
Valley

Yugoslavia

Fodor's Travel Guides

Special Series

Fodor's Affordables

Affordable Europe

Affordable France

Affordable Germany

Affordable Great Britain

Affordable Italy

Fodor's Bed & Breakfast and Country Inns Guides

California

Mid-Atlantic Region

New England

The Pacific Northwest

The South

The West Coast

The Upper Great Lakes Region

Canada's Great Country Inns

Cottages, B&Bs and Country Inns of England and Wales

The Berkeley Guides

On the Loose in California

On the Loose in Eastern Europe

On the Loose in Mexico

On the Loose in the Pacific Northwest & Alaska

Fodor's Exploring Guides

Exploring California

Exploring Florida

Exploring France

Exploring Germany

Exploring Paris

Exploring Rome

Exploring Spain

Exploring Thailand

Fodor's Flashmaps

New York

Washington, D.C.

Fodor's Pocket Guides

Pocket Bahamas

Pocket Jamaica

Pocket London

Pocket New York City

Pocket Paris

Pocket Puerto Rico

Pocket San Francisco

Pocket Washington, D.C.

Fodor's Sports

Cycling

Hiking

Running

Sailing

The Insider's Guide to the Best Canadian Skiing

Fodor's Three-In-Ones (guidebook, language cassette, and phrase book)

France

Germany

Italy

Mexico

Spain

Fodor's Special-Interest Guides

Cruises and Ports of Call

Disney World & the Orlando Area

Euro Disney

Healthy Escapes

London Companion

Skiing in the USA & Canada

Sunday in New York

Fodor's Touring Guides

Touring Europe

Touring USA: Eastern Edition

Touring USA: Western Edition

Fodor's Vacation Planners

Great American Vacations

National Parks of the West

The Wall Street Journal Guides to Business Travel

Europe

International Cities

Pacific Rim

USA & Canada